The
West Dorset
Guide Book

Including Weymouth & The Isle of Portland

by Charles Tait

ISBN 9781909036321

The West Dorset Guide Book

First Edition
©copyright Charles Tait 2015
Published by Charles Tait
Kelton, St Ola, Orkney KW15 1TR
Tel 01856 873738 Fax 01856 875313
charles.tait@zetnet.co.uk
charles-tait.co.uk

Text, design and layout copyright Charles Tait, all photographs copyright Charles Tait unless otherwise credited, old photographs from Charles Tait collection.

OS maps reproduced from Ordnance Survey mapping with permission of the Controller of HMSO, Crown Copyright Reserved 100035677

Printing   by   Martins   the   Printers

The West Dorset

Guide Book
Including Weymouth &
The Isle of Portland

by Charles Tait

This book is dedicated to Gwynedd Short

ACKNOWLEDGEMENTS

During the years of work on the research, photography, design and production of *The West Dorset Guide Book* many people, books, websites, publications and bodies have been consulted. The author

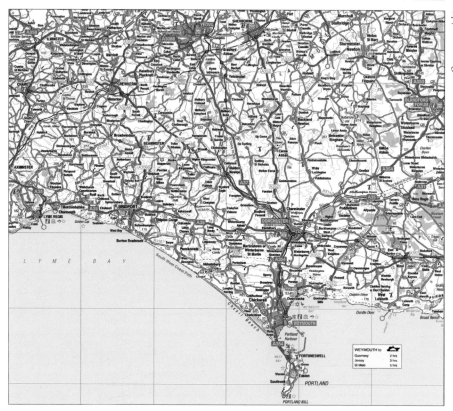

West Dorset stretches from Lyme Regis in the southwest to Sherborne in the north and to Ringstead Bay in the southeast. It is the largest adminstrative district, covering 41% of the county, but holds only 13% of the population.

It includes the county town of Dorchester (19,060), Bridport (13,568), Lyme Regis (3,671), Beaminster (3,136) and Sherborne (9,523) as well as many small attractive villages. Because of its complex geology, West Dorset offers a diversity of landscapes and seascapes. The coastline forms part of the Jurassic Coast World Heritage Site. It includes spectacular beaches, fast eroding clay and sandstone cliffs as well as one of the longest barrier beaches in the world, Chesil Beach.

Administrative districts of Dorset

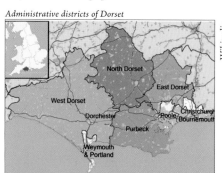

Midwinter sunrise from Charmouth Beach

Marshwood Vale from Pilsdon Pen

The Origin of the Name "Dorset"

Dorset's longest river, the Frome has its source near Evershot. At 30mi (48km) it is the longest chalk stream in the southwest. A large flood plain east of Dorchester was formerly marshy and may give the origin of the British tribe, the *Durotiges* (B water dwellers). The River Piddle rises from a spring at Alton Pancras (OE *awul tun*, source village) and runs for 21mi (30km) before merging with the Frome at Wareham.

There are several shorter rivers, including the Lim, Char, Brit, Bride, Cerne and Wey. "Winterbornes" are common. These are streams which arise from springs in chalk and limestone which only flow after heavy rain has raised the water table sufficiently.

Inland the country is mostly rolling low hills, intersected by lush green valleys. Dorset was once heavily forested but apart from many small relict woodlands, some of which are ancient, it is mostly now pasture. Away from the main roads, the narrow hedge-lined lanes often follow very old routes.

There are many archaeological sites, but by far the most prominent are the Iron Age hill forts. Of these, Maiden Castle is the most spectacular of all. Others include Abbotsbury, Lambert's and Coney's Castles, Pilson Pen and Eggardon Hill.

West Dorset retains many unspoilt natural habitats, partly because of the low population density, lack of industrial development and intensive farming. As a result there are many fascinating sites for those interested in natural history to visit. These range from coastal marshes, unimproved meadows, ancient woodlands to shingle beaches, chalk downlands and heathlands.

The many highly varied nature reserves scattered throughout West Dorset harbour a great variety of species which are rare or threatened elsewhere in Great Britain. These include birds such as the Dartford Warbler, the Red Squirrel, rare reptiles, 46 species of butterflies and many dragonflies. Plant include 10 species of orchids and a further 570 other kinds of wild flowers.

Although Dorset is mentioned in the *Anglo-Saxon Chronicle* in AD891, the root name is very much older. Many variations occur, but all include the prefix dorn, (B *durno-*, large round pebble or fist). The Romans called Dorchester *Durnovaria*, most likely from the original local name. Maiden Castle, the large Iron Age fort 1.6mi (2.5km) southwest of Dorchester may be the *Dunium* (B *dun*, fort) referred to by Ptolemy c.AD150 as the main stronghold of the *Durotriges*.

Interestingly, over 40,000 sling shot pebbles were found at Maiden Castle when excavated. Whether this has anything to do with the name is unknown, but it adds to the mystery.

The Roman name was probably pronounced as *Dornawara* by the locals. Later, the Saxons added a suffix (OE *ceaster*, town) to give *Dornwaraceaster*, soon shortened to Dorchester. This led to the local people being referred to as the *Dornsæte* (OE *sæte*, people), and hence to the modern Dorset.

Perhaps one of the biggest attractions of West Dorset is its timeless quality. The industrial revolution, urbanisation and even modern farming have largely failed to make much impression on this delightful area. Motorways have bypassed it too, making it an even more desirable place to visit. Here it is easy to get away from the rush of modern Britain to a calmer world.

Welcome to West Dorset - A Dramatic Coast

Lyme Regis

Charmouth Beach and Golden Cap at low tide

View east from Golden Cap

West Bay has a shingle beach and spectacular cliffs

The Dorset Coastline offers spectacular options for visitors. The dramatic Jurassic Coast stretches for 95mi (155km) from Exmouth in Devon to Old Harry Rocks at the east end of Purbeck.

Sea Temperatures at Weymouth peak around 18.5°C in early September, which is very pleasant for swimming. In July, August and September they exceed 16°C. In January and February they dip to 4°C.

Lyme Regis has a fine sandy beach, sheltered by the Cobb breakwater. It is a small version of the traditional seaside resort ideal for families. To the west of the harbour Monmouth's Beach is mostly shingle, but is excellent for fossils.

Charmouth also has an excellent fine sandy beach, which stretches for over 2.5mi (4km) all the way to Golden Cap. It is highly variable, sometimes being more shingle than sand. At low tide extensive ledges are revealed. The Charmouth Heritage Coast Centre has fossil displays and runs fossil hunting walks.

Chesil Beach is a massive shingle barrier beach stretching for 18mi (29km) from West Bay to Portland. The size of the pebbles gradually increases from west to east. The shingle makes for hard walking, but the beach can be accessed at many points including West Bay, West Bexington, Abbotsbury and Ferrybridge.

Weymouth became a fashionable seaside resort for rich Georgians in the late 18th century. Today it is an attractive holiday resort town with a beautiful sandy beach that extends around Weymouth Bay for 2.2mi (3.5km). All of the traditional things are on offer including donkey rides, seaside attractions and fish and chips.

Chesil Beach and The Fleet from west of Abbotsbury

The Isle of Portland is joined to Weymouth by Chesil Beach. This resistant limestone outcrop has high cliffs. There are many old quarries; several are nature reserves famous for rare butterflies and wild flowers. Portland Bill is the most southerly point of Dorset.

Weymouth Beach and Esplanade

The White Nothe overlooks Weymouth Bay from the east and marks the start of the Isle of Purbeck limestone and chalk cliffs. From here to the Old Harry Rocks along the South West Coast Path is 30mi (48km). This part of the Jurassic Coast consists of dramatic chalk and limestone cliffs with lovely bays, sea stacks, natural arches and other features. This area is covered in the companion Purbeck Guide.

Chesil Beach from Portland Heights

Ringstead Bay

Best Ten Beaches and Cliffs	
Lyme Regis	20
Charmouth	24
Golden Cap	25, 26
Seatown	27
Eype's Mouth	35
West Bay	34
Burton & Cogden Beach	38
Chesil Beach, The Fleet	39, 76
Weymouth	72
Portland	82
Ringstead Bay	79

Dorset County Museum

Thomas Hardy's Cottage

Athelhampton House

Abbotsbury

Visitor Attractions West Dorset has a huge number of visitor attractions, from internationally important museums to tiny village heritage centres. Many more are included in the Gazetteer and the Information Pages at the back of the book.

Dorchester, the county town of Dorset, makes a good starting point, especially the County Museum with its displays covering fossils, archaeology and history. Along with Maiden Castle, the mighty Iron Age hillforts and Roman remains, there is much to see here.

Thomas Hardy was born in 1840 in a cob and thatch cottage in Higher Bockhampton which was built by his grandfather. Hardy designed the house at Max Gate, situated just east of the town off the A35 bypass road. He lived and worked here from 1885 until his death. Today both houses belong to the National Trust.

Athelhampton House, a 15th century manor houses, is considered to be one of the best in the country. The interior roof of the Great Hall is original and spectacular. Its formal gardens cover 8ha, enclosed in a loop of the River Piddle. The house is signposted off the A35, east of Puddletown, 5mi (8km) from Dorchester.

Abbotsbury is situated at the north end of The Fleet, facing Chesil Beach. Its Swannery, Sub-Tropical Gardens, attractive old thatched stone cottages and situation make it a very attractive village. St Catherine's Chapel offers fine views over Chesil Beach to Portland.

The Cerne Giant is on the A352 between Dorchester and Sherborne. This enigmatic tumescent man, with a large club, is cut out of the chalk on a hillside above Cerne Abbas on the A352 north of Dorchester. He may date from Roman times.

The Cene Giant

Sherborne is said to be *"the most attractive town in the county."* Its many lovely old buildings include the Abbey, founded in 705, the Norman Old Castle and the New Castle, first built by Sir Walter Raleigh. The unspoilt town centre has many interesting shops and is situated 20mi (32km) northwest of Dorchester.

Sherborne Abbey

Tolpuddle Martyrs Museum tells the story of six farmworkers who were sentenced to transportation to Australia in 1834 for forming a secret society. They were pardoned in 1836 and the events are now seen as the foundation of trade unions.

The Nothe Fort, Weymouth

The Nothe Fort at Weymouth is part of Portland Harbour, which was developed as a huge naval base. the fort is the most impressive military structure in Dorset. A coast defence fort was established here in the 15th century and hugely enlarged in the 1860s. It only went out of use during the Cold War. The fort has many interesting exhibits from various eras.

Tolpuddle Martyrs' Museum

BEST TEN VISITOR ATTRACTIONS	
Abbotsbury	38
Athelhampton House	66
Cerne Giant	44
Dorchester	54
Dorset County Museum	56
Hardy's Cottage	62
Nothe Fort	80
Sherborne Abbey	50
Sherbourne Castles	48
Tolpuddle Martyrs	68

The Grey Mare and Her Colts

The Nine Stones

Ancient Dorset There are a vast number of archaeological and prehistorical sites in Dorset. Many were dug into in the 19th century by gentlemen antiquarians and some have been more scientifically excavated in modern times.

Very few such places are signposted or presented to the public to visit. To many this simply increases the challenge and satisfaction of finding and experiencing ancient sites.

Throughout the book Ordnance Survey coordinates are quoted to aid visitors.

Palaeolithic Age The first evidence of people in Dorset is handaxes dating from at least 400,000 years ago found in gravel deposits beside rivers. There are no sites to visit, but the County Museum un Dorchester has exhibits.

Mesolithic Age At the start of the last inter-glacial period around 11,000BC people started to arrive over the land bridge to Europe as the climate warmed up. They left many traces of shelters, hearths and piles of shells, including at Culverwell near Portland Bill.

Neolithic Age Dorset has many remains from the time of the first farmers from c.4000BC onwards. These include causewayed camps, burial mounds, enclosures, ditches and banks. They also built henges, some of which were huge. Sadly only vestiges of these remain. Pottery as well as stone and bone tools can be seen in the museums.

Bronze Age There are funerary barrows, dating from c.2000BC and later, all over the county. Some yielded exceptionally rich grave goods when dug into in the 19th century.

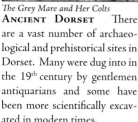

The Valley of the Stones

Maiden Castle ramparts

Roman Town House mosaics

Eggardon Iron Age hillfort

There are remains of farms, field systems and settlements in many areas, especially in the Valley of the Stones. Barrows are especially evident beside the A35 between Dorchester and Bridport.

Iron Age Starting c.6000BC hillforts were constructed in large numbers all over Dorset, some on the site of previous Neolithic enclosures such as at Maiden Castle. They vary in size and complexity but all are hilltops defended by massive ramparts and ditches and enclose roundhouse settlements. Eggardon Hill as well as Abbotsbury, Coney's and Lamberts Castles are good examples in West Dorset.

The Romans rapidly took over the whole of southern England after their invasion of AD43, including Dorset. Their roads are still very prominent in the landscape, especially around Dorchester. Villas, mosaics, temples, aqueducts, town wall, forts, harbours, weapons, tools, pottery and household artefacts have all been found. The County Museum has a good display of Roman artefacts.

The Saxons took control of Dorset by the late 7th century. By the end of the 9th century Wessex was fully established under Alfred the Great. Abbeys such as Sherborne and Abbotsbury were founded and many churches were built. A number of retain some Saxon features, such as doorways, carved stones and crosses.

The Normans, who were really Vikings masquerading as Frenchmen took over a highly organised country in 1066.

Dorset has many churches and abbeys built by them, usually on the site of earlier Saxon chapels. There are only a very few ruined castles from this time, most having long since fallen out of use and been demolished. Sherborne Abbey was remodelled by the Normans, while they also built the Old Castle in the 12th century.

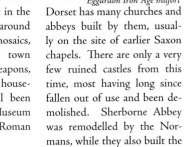

Whitcombe Church

BEST TEN HISTORICAL SITES	
Dorchester	54
Dorset County Museum	56
Eggardon Hill	42
Grey Mare & Her Colts	40
Kingston Russell Circle	40
Maiden Castle	64
The Nine Stones	40
Sherborne Castle & Abbey	48
Valley of the Stones	40
Whitcombe Church	67

Sherborne Abbey

Nature and Environment

Wootton Fitzpaine meadow

Bluebell woodland

Green-winged Orchids at Wootton Fitzpaine

Powerstock Common has disused railway line

Dorset has many superb places to find wildlife. Apart from the famous and varied coastline, there are a host of nature reserves and other wild places, some remote, others right in the middle of towns.

West Dorset's unspoilt wild flower-filled meadows are a delight. At Wootton Fitzpaine, Powerstock Common and Kingcombe Meadows, among other places, these present a continuously changing kaleidescope of colour from early spring through summer.

Orchids including Green-winged, Bee, Pyramidal and Autumn Ladies Tresses are locally common in unimproved meadows. First Snowdrops, then Wood Anemones followed by Bluebells, carpet woodland areas while the roadside verges and hedges present an ever changing spectacle.

Ancient hillforts, such as Coney's or Lambert's Castles and Eggardon Hill are botanical delights and good for birds too. Chalk downland valleys such as Lankham Bottom or Hog Cliff harbour rare butterflies and wild flowers.

Cogden Beach, near Burton Bradstock, is of shingle, backed by sand, dune slacks and old meadows at the western extremity of Chesil Beach. Burton Mere, a small fresh water pond, is surrounded by marsh and reeds. The whole area is a magnet for migrant birds and harbours many rare plants.

Radipole Lake and Lodmoor Reserves in central Weymouth are wetland RSPB reserves. Bearded Tits, Cetti's Warblers, Marsh Harriers, Bitterns and Kingfishers may be seen here along with many wildfowl and common species of birds.

Butterflies and dragonflies are abundant in summer. Otters and Water Vole are present along with Eels and many other fish as well as Frogs and Toads.

Portland Quarries which are no longer used for stone extraction are now nature reserves. These include Broadcroft and Tout Quarries, which harbour a special range of limestone-loving wild flowers. In turn these attract a number of butterflies rarely seen elsewhere.

Portland Bill, with its Bird Observatory, is internationally known as a migrant bird recording site due to its position on the English Channel. The lighthose offers spectacular views along the Dorset coast. The rocks here are full of fossils, mostly molluscs

Cogden Beach

Radipole RSPB Reserve

Tout Quarry Nature Reserve

Portland Bill

BEST TEN NATURE SITES	
Cogden Beach	38
Coney's Castle	28
Eggardon Hill	42
Kingcombe Meadows	43
Lankham Bottom	46
Lyme Bay	20
Portland	90
Powerstock Common	42
Radipole Lake	77
The Fleet	39

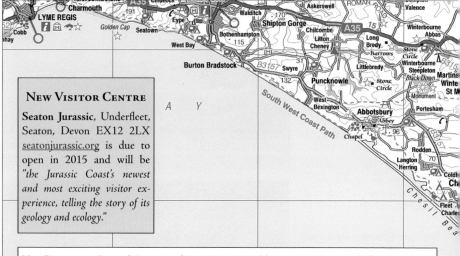

New Visitor Centre

Seaton Jurassic, Underfleet, Seaton, Devon EX12 2LX seatonjurassic.org is due to open in 2015 and will be *"the Jurassic Coast's newest and most exciting visitor experience, telling the story of its geology and ecology."*

The "Jurassic Coast" Dorset and East Devon World Heritage Site extends for about 95mi (155km) from Orcombe Point near Exmouth in Devon to Old Harry Rocks near Swanage in Purbeck, Dorset. It was inscribed by UNESCO in 2001 on account of its exposures of the geology of the Mesozoic Period.

The World Heritage Site is a narrow strip of coastline stretching from the lowest spring ebb to the tops of the adjacent cliffs. Known as the "Jurassic Coast", it includes exposures from the whole of the Mesozoic Period, including the Triassic (252-201Ma, Jurassic (201-145Ma) and Cretaceous (145-66Ma) Periods.

Lyme Regis The middle section of the Jurassic Coast has many spectacular features. Between Lyme Regis and Charmouth Beach landslides from the quickly eroding cliffs regularly release fossils onto the shoreline. The best time to seek them is after heavy rain on a falling spring tide.

Ammonites and belemnites are the most frequent finds, but vertebrae from Ichthyosaurs and other marine reptiles may also be discovered. Fossil plants and insects, such as dragonflies, are also present. Preserved footprints of dinosaurs and tree stumps also occur.

Golden Cap (191m) is the highest point on the south coast. Topped by Greensand, this elegantly eroding headland affords spectacular views from Portland in the east to Start Point in the west. High cliffs, subject to landslips, continue past Seatown to Eype's Mouth.

Charmouth Beach and Golden Cap at low tide

East Cliff at West Bay

Portland West Coast

The Fleet and Chesil Beach

All along this coast from Lyme Regis to Burton Bradstock, deep valleys have been gouged out by ancient rivers, which have equally old names such as Lim, Char, Brit and Bride. Lyme Regis, Charmouth, Chideock, Seatown, Bridport and Burton Bradstock all shelter in these valleys.

Cliffs From Eype east to Burton the coastline becomes spectacular vertical sandstone cliffs, up to 50m high. Some beaches are sandy in places but most are shingle and pebbles, which increase in size towards the east. Rockfalls happen regularly, sadly tragically sometimes with fatal consequences.

Chesil Beach Cogden Beach marks the west end of Chesil Beach, a massive barrier beach c.18mi (28km) long. It encloses the Fleet, a long sheltered lagoon, with fresh water in the west and open to the sea in the east. It was probably formed by the build up of pebbles caused by the prevailing westerly wind and sea.

The Isle of Portland is composed of fine-grained Oolitic Limestone, an excellent masonry stone. The west coast has ruggedly beautiful cliffs, while inland are many quarries, some still worked. Near Portland Bill, the most southerly point in Dorset, a raised beach marks former higher sea levels.

Ammonite

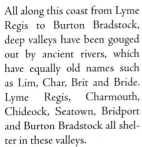

Ichthyosaur

JURASSIC COAST LYME TO PORTLAND	
Lyme Regis	20
Charmouth	24
Golden Cap	25, 26
Seatown	27
Eype's Mouth	35
West Bay	34
Burton Beach	38
Cogden Beach	38
Chesil Beach, The Fleet	38, 39
Ferry Bridge	76
Portland	82

Ammonite fossil on Charmouth Beach at low tide

Administrative districts of Dorset

WEST DORSET stretches from Lyme Regis in the southwest to Sherborne in the north and to Ringstead Bay in the southeast. It is the largest adminstrative district of Dorset, covering 41% of the county, but holds only 13% of the population.

Towns and Villages It includes the county town of Dorchester (popn 2011, 19,060), Bridport (popn 2011, 13,568), Lyme Regis (popn, 2011 3,671), Beaminster (popn 2011, 3,136) and Sherborne (popn, 2011 9,523). There are many attractive small villages.

Coastline The West Dorset coastline extends to about 40mi (60km) by footpath and is part of the Jurassic Coast World Heritage Site. With spectacular cliffs, beautiful beaches and good access this coast is a delight to explore.

Inland West Dorset offers much to the visitor, including many hillforts and nature reserves harbouring rare birds, butterflies and wildflowers.

Weymouth (B *Wey* OE *mūða*, Mouth of the River Wey, popn. 52,323 in 2011) is today an attractive holiday resort town. Its beautiful wide sandy beach extends for 2.2mi (3.5km) around Weymouth Bay.

The Isle of Portland (OE *port land*, land sheltering the port, popn 2011, 12,844) is oined to the mainland by the shingle barrier of Chesel Beach. It is about 4mi (6km) long.

WEST DORSET	
Abbotsbury	38
Batcombe	47
Beaminster	28
Blackmore Vale	48
Bridport	30
Burton Bradstock	38
Cerne Giant	44
Charmouth	24
Chesil Beach	38
Chideock	26
Colmer's Hill	27
Compton Valence	43
Coney's Castle	28
Eggardon Hill	42
Evershot	46
Eype's Mouth	35
Forde Abbey	29
Golden Cap	25, 26
Hardy's Monument	41
Hellstone	40
Kingcombe Meadows	43
Kingston Russell Circle	40
Lambert's Castle	28
Lankham Bottom	46
Lyme Regis	20
Mangerton Mill	33
Mapperton House	29
Mare & Her Colts	40
Marshwood Vale	28
Melbury Bubb	47
Minterne Gardens	45
Nine Stones	40
Pilsdon Pen	28
Portesham	41
Powerstock Common	42
Roman Road	42, 54
Seatown	27
Sherborne	48
Stonebarrow Hill	24
The Fleet	39
Valley of the Stones	40
West Bay	34
West Bexington	38
Whitchurch	26
Wootton Fitzpaine	25
Yetminster	47

LYME REGIS

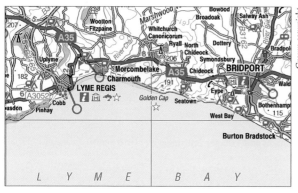

LYME REGIS (B *Lim*, stream, 2011 population, 3,671) is situated in a prime position at the west end of Lyme Bay, sheltered from the west and north. In 774 Sherborne Abbey was granted rights to salt-panning here by Saxon King Cynewulf.

By the 12th century Lyme was a substantial fishing port and trading with France. As one of the few harbours between Exmouth and Weymouth, in all probability it had been a sea port since early times.

The Cobb (OE *cobb*, cobble) was originally constructed from large oak piles, which enclosed a mass of large stones. It suffered storm damage in 1328, but may well be much older than that. The Cobb was not joined to the land until 1690 and has sustained damage from heavy seas on many occasions. The present structure dates from the 1790s with later additions in the 1820s.

"Regis" was added in 1384, when Lyme was granted a Royal Charter by Edward I. It became one of England's major ports, trading with France, shipbuilding, fishing and smuggling all playing their part. As ships grew in size it declined in importance by the late 18th century.

The Cobb has an extension of Norwegian granite to shelter pontoons and moorings for visiting yachts. The inner harbour is protected by the eastern breakwater, complete with old cannons. The Old Pier has a marine aquarium and is the departure point for fishing and sight seeing boat trips.

Siege During the Civil War, Lyme was besieged by the Royalists from 20th April to 15th June 1644. Under Prince Maurice, a nephew of Charles I, 6,000 Royalists attacked

MARY ANNING

Mary Anning (1799-1847) made many significant discoveries of *Ichthyosaurs, Plesiosaurs* and other prehistoric reptile species. The coast here is unstable and subject to frequent landslips, which have the benefit of revealing many fossils from the Jurassic Blue Lias rocks.

Her background and gender made her unable to participate fully in the scientific community, but she became an expert in fossils and geology. She resented this, saying that, "*the world has used her ill ... these men of learning have sucked her brains, and made a great deal of publishing works, of which she furnished the contents, while she derived none of the advantages.*" Today she is considered to be a key figure in 19th century geology.

Mary Anning and her dog

Sketch of an Ichthyosaur fossil found and reassembled by Mary Anning

Lyme seafront from Langmoor Gardens

the town. The defence was led by Colonel Robert Blake and greatly aided by supplies shipped in by sea.

The townswomen played a crucial role, building and manning earthworks, digging trenches and reloading guns. Roofs were stripped of their thatch in response to fire arrows and red hot cannon balls that rained down on the town. Eventually the Royalists withdrew, having sustained over 2,000 casualties. Prince Maurice's reputation never recovered from being defeated by *"this vile fishing town defended by a dry ditch."*

Lyme Regis Museum was built in 1901 near where the Anning's shop once stood.

Big waves breaking over the Cobb during a storm and exceptionally high tide

Thomas Hollis

THOMAS HOLLIS

Thomas Hollis (1720-74) was a political philosopher and supporter of American republicanism. Having been left considerable wealth, he reprinted many books and published works by American colonists. He was a benefactor to a great number of libraries, in Britain, Europe and America, especially Harvard.

Hollis had a 3000-acre estate at Corscombe, northeast of Beaminster, to which he retired in 1770. He took a great interest in the development of Lyme Regis as a resort and bought up considerable areas of the town for redevelopment. Among his projects were the promenade, now Marine Parade, and the Assembly Halls.

Boats moored in the sheltered inner harbour

Broad Street from an old postcard

Broad Street with the Three Cups and Royal Lion Hotels

Sir George Somers

Sir George Somers (1554-1610) is regarded as the founder of the Colony of Bermuda. He is commemorated on a large plaque on the Cobb. Born in Lyme Regis, he had a successful career in the Navy Royal, before leading a re-supply fleet to the new colony of Jamestown in 1609. His ship, *Sea Venture*, was wrecked on Bermuda but everyone reached their destination eventually.

Somers returned to Bermuda in 1610 to collect supplies, but died there. His heart was buried at St Georges, which is now twinned with Lyme Regis, while his pickled body was returned for burial with full military honours at Whitchurch Canonicorum. Each April a group from Lyme visits St Georges and a return party comes over during Lifeboat Week in July.

It has collections of fossils, artefacts, photographs and artwork from the area. The building has small rooms, a winding staircase and a later glass-walled addition. Nearby, an old chapel dating from 1755 houses Dinosaurland, which has more locally-found fossils and several replica dinosaurs.

The Town Mill is said to date from 1340. The restored workings again grind flour, from local grain, by water power. Part of it is now a microbrewery producing a range of beers in its 72 firkin (652l) four barrel brew length tanks.

The Undercliff runs from Monmouth Beach westwards to Axmouth. A 5mi (8km) path leads through this overgrown area. In 1839 a huge landslip occurred at Dowlands where a section about 0.75mi (1.25km) wide moved 90m.

The Spittles lie to the east of the town. This area is very unstable and is slowly slipping into the sea. Major works have been in progress in recent years to stabilise the gardens above Marine Parade and, more recently, to the east of the town.

Sir George Somers

Chart of Bermuda surveyed by Sir George Somers

Monmouth Beach to the west of the Cobb is where the Duke of Monmouth and his party landed at the start of their abortive coup in June 1685. This led to the hanging, disembowelment and butchery of hundreds of participants, and the transportation of many more. The ferocity of James II and his "hanging" Judge Jeffries led to the "Glorious Revolution" of 1688.

Marine Parade from an old postcard

Tourism Since the 1780s Lyme Regis has been a popular holiday destination, on account of its fine beach and attractive situation. The town has had many distinguished literary visitors and residents over the years, all perhaps attracted by the fine location and peaceful environment. They have greatly aided its development as a popular visitor destination over the years.

Literary Visitors One of the first was Jane Austen (1775-1817) who visited in 1803 and 1804 with her family. Her description is very apt today, *"The scenes in its neighbourhood, Charmouth, with its high grounds and extensive sweeps of country, and still more, its sweet, retired bay, backed by dark cliffs, where fragments of low rock among the sands, make it the happiest spot for watching the flow of the tide, for sitting in unwearied contemplation; the woody varieties of the cheerful village of Up Lyme; and, above all, Pinny, with its green chasms between romantic rocks, where the scattered forest trees and*

orchards of luxuriant growth, declare that many a generation must have passed away since the first partial falling of the cliff prepared the ground for such a state, where a scene so wonderful and so lovely is exhibited, as may more than equal any of the resembling scenes of the far-famed Isle of Wight: these places must be visited, and visited again, to make the worth of Lyme understood."

Today Lyme has much to offer the visitor, whether staying for some days or just a few hours. The sea front with its splendid views, sandy or shingle beaches and Marine Parade are perhaps its essence. There is a wide range of interesting shops and attractions as well as many places to stay, eat and drink.

Jane Austen

Seafood Lovers should not miss the Hix Oyster & Fish House, which overlooks the harbour in Lyme Regis. *"This is easily one of the most picturesque spots to enjoy fresh seafood. The focus is on sourcing and serving the best produce we can find and doing as little to it as possible so that you enjoy the real flavour of great British ingredients.*

Christmas illuminations in Lyme

Charmouth Beach and Lyme Bay in 1822

CHARMOUTH (B *Cerne, carn,* gravel, stony OE *mūde,* mouth, *Cernemude*) is an attractive village situated on a hill above Lyme Bay. Now bypassed by the A35, it was on the Roman road which can still be found on the ridge north of the village at Hogchester (OE *hogg hyrst,* pig farm on wooded hill).

Apart from its excellent selection of local shops and holiday accommodation, the main feature of Charmouth is the beach, with its dramatic eroding cliffs. Unusually the foreshore here belongs to the village and not the Crown Estate.

This beach is one of the best places on the Jurassic Coast to look for fossils. The most common are ammonites and belemnites which get washed out of the collapsing cliffs and also may be found at low tide. A nearly complete *Ichthyosaur* fossil was found on 26th December 2013 below the Black Ven. It is about 1.5m long and the best example found in recent years.

Charmouth Heritage Coast Centre is based in an old cement factory above the beach. It has a large collection of fossils, as well as displays on geology and wildlife. It runs fossil hunting walks and welcomes many school trips every year.

The beach stretches 2.5mi (4km) east to Golden Cap and about 1.5mi (2.5km) west to Lyme Regis. At low tide a large area of sand and rocks is exposed. The beach is highly variable depending on the weather, sometimes being nearly all sand and at other times all shingle. *Care should be taken to check the tide times to avoid becoming stranded.*

Stonebarrow Hill (186m) overlooks Charmouth from the east. Reached by Stonebarrow Lane from the east of the village, there is a car park and a seasonal National Trust Visitor Centre at the top. There are excellent panoramic views over Lyme Bay from here. Footpaths criss-cross

Charmouth Beach from the St Gabriel's Steps, east of Stonebarrow Hill

Charmouth Beach at low tide with Golden Cap in the distance

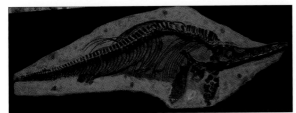
Fossil Ichthyosaur in Charmouth Heritage Coast Centre

the area to Golden Cap and beyond. A fine circular walk starts at the Heritage Centre and follows the beach for 2mi (3km) eastwards to St Gabriel's Steps. After exploring St Gabriel's Chapel climb to the top of Golden Cap and return via Langdon Hill and Stonebarrow Hill 4mi (6km).

Wootton Fitzpaine (OE *wudu tūn*, Wood Farm) lies just inland from Charmouth, set in rolling country with many hedge-lined lanes. Its meadows and woodlands have lovely displays of wild Daffodils,

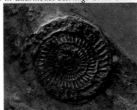
Large ammonite on the beach

Cowslips, Wood Anemones, Bluebells, Green-winged and other Orchids. The verges here seem to have a never-ending display of flora from late January until November. Perhaps spring is the best time to take a walk around the lanes here.... or summer, or autumn.

Charmouth from an old postcard

The Street, Charmouth today

Golden Cap affords fine views towards Portland in the east

WHITCHURCH (OE *Witas cirice*, Wita's Church, after St Wita or St Candida, a Saxon holy woman who was traditionally martyred by Vikings) This is the only English parish church where a shrine with its saint's relics survived the Reformation.

The shrine is a simple altar tomb with three oval openings and a top of Purbeck Marble. Inside the coffin a lead reliquary contains some bone and the inscription "*XT REQUE SCE W HIC REQUESCT SCT WITE*", "*Here rest the remains of St Wite*". The water from nearby St Wite's Well has long been thought to have been a cure for sore eyes. Periwinkles are called "*St Candida's Eyes*" in this area.

Sir George Somers, who colonised Bermuda, is buried here. There is a prominent brass plaque and a copy of his portrait in the church. He was interred with full military honours in 1611. Other more recent incumbents include the murdered Bulgarian dissident, Georgi Markov and the broadcaster, Sir Robin Day.

Golden Cap (SY405921, 191m) is the highest point on the south coast. The cliff is topped by a layer of gleaming yellow Greensand which makes it stand out as a landmark for miles around. It can be reached by footpath from Charmouth via Stonebarrow Hill, from a carpark at Langdon Wood, west of Chideock or by the coastal path from Seatown.

The headland offers a spectacular view of Lyme Bay from Portland in the east to Start Point in the far west. Golden Cap is an excellent place to look out for migratory birds in spring and autumn.

Chideock (B *cēdīog*, Wooded Place) is a small village to the west of Bridport whose ambience is ruined by the lack of

St Wite's Well

Seatown Beach with Ridge Cliff in the background

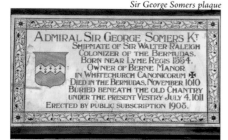
Sir George Somers plaque

ADMIRAL SIR GEORGE SOMERS KT
SHIPMATE OF SIR WALTER RALEIGH
COLONIZER OF THE BERMUDAS.
BORN NEAR LYME REGIS 1554.
OWNER OF BERNE MANOR
IN WHITECHURCH CANONICORUM ✠
DIED IN THE BERMUDAS, NOVEMBER 1610
BURIED BENEATH THE OLD CHANTRY
UNDER THE PRESENT VESTRY JULY 4, 1611
ERECTED BY PUBLIC SUBSCRIPTION 1908.

St Wite's shrine, Whitchurch

Hollow way near Symondsbury

Colmer's Hill

a bypass. The A35 thunders right through what could be a lovely tranquil place. Although a new main road was planned, vested interests have consigned a pretty village to traffic misery.

Around 1380 Chideock Castle was built just to the north of the village. This estate was eventually acquired by the Catholic Arundell family, who protected priests and others from persecution under Henry VIII and Elizabeth I. The Chideock Martyrs were tried and executed in 1594 for their Catholic faith. In all, around 360 people were put to death between 1535 and 1681 for being of the Catholic faith.

During the Civil War, Chideock Castle was in Royalist hands, but was ultimately destroyed in 1645 by Parliamentary forces. Today a

wooden cross in memory of the Martyrs stands over part of the moat. In 1874 the present church next to the Manor House was completed. A small museum attached to it has an eclectic collection of artefacts ranging from Civil War cannonballs to items washed up on Seatown Beach.

A gateway at Chideock Manor has the jawbones of a large baleen whale set up like an archway. These are probably from either a Blue or a Fin Whale, but their provenance is now unknown.

Seatown is, in contrast, a haven of tranquillity, reached by a side road from Chideock. Here there are lovely views along the cliffs in both directions, as well as a fine shingle beach. There are also fine walks along the Coastal Path to West Bay, via

Eype and to Charmouth via Golden Cap. The Anchor Inn is a welcoming old pub, providing good food and refreshment.

Colmer's Hill, with its lonely pine trees is a prominent viewpoint to the north of the A35 approaching Bridport. It can be reached by a path from Symondsbury which leads up one of the many ancient hollow ways in this area. These sunken trackways often lead into little visited and mysterious places, close to civilisation and yet strangely remote.

Whalebone archway, Chideock

Site of Chideock Castle

Chideock has many thatched houses

Marshwood Vale & Beaminster

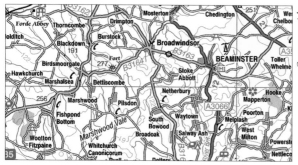

tower from the 16th. Tradition has it that people were hanged from the tower and left to rot. In the town square an imposing market house monument erected in 1906 to one Julia Robinson takes pride of place. There are many interesting and attractive buildings around the market square and in the side streets around it.

Beaminster Tunnel was opened in 1832. It carries the A3066 under Horn Hill, just north of the town. At 105m long, it avoided the very steep hill, a problem for horse-drawn traffic. It is the last remaining operational road tunnel in the country to predate the railways.

Coney's Castle has impressive drifts of Bluebells in springtime

MARSHWOOD VALE (OE *mersc wudu*, marshy wood) is a large valley formed from relatively impermeable Lower Lias clay. This made it very marshy in wet weather before drainage schemes. Here, narrow lanes, lined by hedges wind around small fields. Areas of woodland persist, some ancient.

Lambert's Castle

Beaminster (OE *Bēage mynster*, Bēage's church, popn. 2011, 3,136) is an attractive small town 5mi (8km) north of Bridport. It was largely destroyed by the Royalists in 1644 and again by accident in 1684 and 1781. As a result most of the town dates from rebuilding in limestone with tiled roofs in the late 18th and early 19th centuries.

St Mary's Church dates from the 15th century and its fine tall

Beaminster is mostly built of local limestone

Pilsdon Pen (OE *piles dūn*, Peaked Hill B *penn*, hill, 277m) is the largest of several hillforts which dominate the area. Most of the villages around the Vale are on higher ground. Second in size only to Maiden Castle in Dorset, this defensive site dominates the landscape for miles around.

Lambert's Castle (256m) is a large, tree-covered hillfort to the north of Wootton Fitzpaine on the B3185 over-

Pilsdon Pen has a large, dramatic hillfort and affords panoramic views over Marshwood Vale to the coast

looking Marshwood Vale. Just to the south, Coney's Castle is bisected by a side road. In April it has some of the best displays of Bluebells in Dorset.

Broadwindsor is situated in a deep valley between Lewesdon Hill (279m) and Conegar Hill. It is named from the windlass that was formerly used to help carts up the steep hill. It offers fine views of Pilsdon Pen.

Waddon Hill (207m, ST448015) has a ruined Roman fort which was occupied during 50-60AD. Artefacts may be seen in Bridport Museum.

Lewesdon Hill (279m) is the highest point in Dorset. Like Pilsdon Pen, it is formed from erosion resistant Upper Greensand and has a hillfort, now hidden by woodland.

Mapperton House and Gardens, to the east of Beaminster, are open to the public in summer. The 17th century manor is said to be one of the finest in the country, while the attractive gardens were mostly created in the 20th century.

Forde Abbey lies on the Devon border, south of the River Axe. It was only partially complete by the Dissolution in 1539, when it was taken over as a house. Today it is a fascinating mixture of periods and survivals. The gardens have many beautiful trees, which are spectacular in autumn, while in spring vast numbers of Daffodils and Bluebells are a sight to behold.

Thorncombe (ST375033) is a small village on the way to Forde Abbey. The present church was opened in 1867, but includes artefacts from the previous medieval building including a large memorial brass to Sir Thomas and Lady Brooke who died in 1417 and 1437 repectively. He was much in favour with Henry IV and a Member of the Commons.

Beaminster Tunnel opened in 1832

Memorial to Julia Robinson
Forde Abbey has very attractive gardens

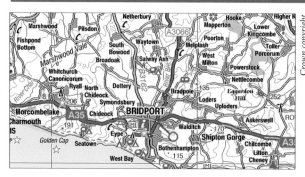

The town subsequently expanded northwards to West and East Streets, which straddle the old Roman road from Dorchester to Exeter. This would have greatly facilitated land communications. The Brit estuary was the only sheltered port on Lyme Bay until the building of the Cobb at Lyme Regis.

BRIDPORT (B River *Bredy* or *Bride* OE *port*, market town, popn. 2011, 13,568) is situated between the Rivers Brit and Asker above their confluence and flood plain. The name may derive from OE *Brydian*, place at the River Bride, the original ancient fortified settlement at Bredy having been abandoned in favour of a better location with sea access.

The River Brit is probably a back-formation as it was originally called the Wooth. Since no evidence of Roman or earlier habitation has been found, it seems that Bridport dates from Saxon times. The first settlement was probably around St Mary's Church at the bottom of South Street. Access to the sea was possible by shallow-draughted craft.

Defences Although no archaeological evidence has been found for a castle or town walls, there are several intriguing placenames. Bridport Museum occupies a 16th century house on the east side of South Street called the Old Castle. Land behind it was called Castlehay, or Castle Field. To the east of the town, in the vicinity of Walditch formerly known as Waldyke are the remains of a stone wall and ditch which may represent an old boundary.

Rope-making The town has been known for its production of ropes and nets since the 13th century. Since Saxon times large amounts of hemp and flax were grown nearby. The first written record is from 1211, when King John ordered quantities of cordage and sails. In 1212 he exhorted that *"..at Bridport, night and day, as many ropes both large and small and as many cables as you can be made..."* (sic).

Henry VIII ordered that all hemp grown within 5 miles of the town was to be used for naval rope making. Rope

Attractive terrace in South Street

West Street from an old postcard

and sail making flourished for many years, despite competition from other areas and the setting up of the Naval Dockyards at Chatham, Plymouth and Portsmouth.

Firms came and went but one of the oldest was Joseph Gundry, established in 1665. Today it is part of AmSafe and specialist nets are still made for fishing, military, sporting, safety, aviation and even space applications. Aircraft products are especially pervasive and include seat belts, cabin furnishings, nets and cargo retainers. Football and tennis nets are also important items.

The "Bridport dagger", was for long slang for the hangman's noose, used to execute his "clients". Hanging was for long the favoured method of execution and Bridport rope was the preferred choice of hangmen for centuries. An example is on display in the museum.

The town's first royal borough charter was granted by Henry III in 1253, since reaffirmed several times by Henry

South Street from near the Town Hall

Attractive old building

The Town Hall clock

St Mary's Church is off South Street

Net making in former times

Bridport Town Hall with Christmas lights

East Street in the 1930s

Bridport Dagger and a 19th century apothecary's store. The museum tells the story of the town from early times, while the Local History Collection holds information on genealogy.

VII and Elizabeth I. Bridport was thus in charge of its commercial affairs from an early date, which contributed much to its economic success.

Old Buildings St Mary's Church dates from the early 13th century. It was renovated and extended in the 14th and 15th centuries and may have been largely complete by 1482. It was built on the site of a much earlier Saxon church.

The Chantry, the oldest building in Bridport, at the south end of South Street, was probably first built in the 13th century. It may have acted as a leading light to Bridport Harbour to help vessels avoid the dangerous reefs in the approach. The building in Bridport was remodelled in c.1370 as a priest's house by

the insertion of fireplaces. It is now an eclectic self catering establishment run by the Landmark Trust.

Bridport Town Hall, situated at the top of South Street, was opened in 1786 as the first manifestation of the Bridport Improvement Act, 1875. The first floor was both Council Chamber and the magistrate's court, while the ground floor had 37 butcher's booths. The new building replaced *"The Shambles"* or Butcher's Row together with the Market House.

Bridport Museum is housed in the "Old Castle", a 16th century building in South Street. The diverse collections include the history of net and rope-making in the town, Roman artefacts from nearby Waddon Hill fort, the story of the

Palmer's Brewery stands at the river confluence, where a waterwheel once provided power. Established in 1714, it belonged to several people before being taken over by Palmer Bros in 1892 and renamed as The Old Brewery. It is said to be the only European brewery with a thatched roof and remains in production today.

Shopping Bridport boasts the UK's oldest continuously trading family business in RJ Balson & Son's Butcher's Shop at West Allington. In 1515 a Balson is recorded as having a butcher's stall in the town, in the vicinity of the present Town Hall.

Other interesting shops include T Snook, "Hatters and Outfitters", Bridport Bookshop, two more butchers' shops, Leakers bakery and a variety of independent jewellers, clothes shops and other

St Mary's Church dates from the 13th century

The Chantry

outlets. The town also retains many local electrical, hardware and other shops.

Most of the buildings date from the late 18th and 19th centuries and are brick-built. Many seemingly new façades only slightly mask interesting old shop fronts and advertisements all of which add colour to the streets. The terraced worker's houses on the east side of South Street present an especially satisfying scene.

Market Today the town has a vibrant street market on Wednesdays and Saturdays. Stalls sell all manner of things from local food produce to clothes and bric a brac. It extends on the pavements of all three main streets. There is a farmer's market once a month.

Arts & Culture The town has a vibrant arts scene. The Lyric Theatre, Electric Palace Cinema and Bridport Arts Centre all host events. Festivals include the Bridport Literary Festival, Book Festival, Food Festival and Hat Festival plus the annual carnival in August. Artists' galleries and antique shops are also a feature.

Mangerton Mill, north of Bridport

Mangerton Mill (SY488958) is situated 2mi (3km) north of Bridport off the A3066 road to Beaminster. This partially restored 17th century water mill is in working order and incorporates a small museum.

There is also a tea room, several craft workshops, a fly fishing lake and a small caravan site. The lake is attractive to waterfowl in winter, while there are pleasant walks along the small River Manger.

T Snook, Hatter & Outfitter

RJ Balson & Sons butcher shop

The Electric Palace

Palmer's Brewery

Millennium carved stonework

Christmas music

West Bay in 1822 from East Cliff by William Daniell

WEST BAY Bridport Harbour, or West Bay, has been in use since the 13th century or earlier. The harbour was redeveloped in the 18th century and saw a huge surge of growth in shipping and ship building which lasted for nearly 150 years. A new harbour was first built in 1744 and by 1760 ships were being built here.

It was only in 1819 that a proper road was built to Bridport, one mile away. By 1824 a new harbour had been built, greatly helping with the development of the rope, net and sail-making industries. Large ships were built here culminating in the "*Speedy*", at 182ft and 1,460tons, the biggest ship ever built at West Bay.

Between 1832 and 1881 Bridport Harbour thrived as a designated Customs bond port. After this the name was changed to West Bay to enhance its attraction to the nascent tourism industry. In 1885 Pier Terrace was built in the Arts and Crafts style.

Recently the harbour has been redeveloped along with massive coastal defences. No longer a commercial port, West Bay is now home to a few fishing boats as well as many pleasure craft and others for hire.

Cliffs & Beaches From West Bay the spectacular coastline of the Jurassic Coast stretches in both directions. The impressive cliffs at East Cliff, Burton Freshwater and Burton Cliff offer panoramic views. The beach towards the east is shingle and forms the westward end of Chesil Beach.

Westwards, West Cliff is equally impressive with vertical sandstone craigs, translating into collapsing banks towards Thorncombe Beacon. All along this coast the landscape keeps changing as does the geology.

Pier Terrace was built in 1885 in Arts & Crafts style

West Bay Beach and East Cliff from the pier

West Bay Harbour

West Bay from East Cliff

Fish & Chips West Bay has several kiosks serving traditional fish and chips, which vie with each other to be the best in the southwest. There are also several good seafood restaurants and pubs at West Bay as well as an excellent fish shop.

Eype's Mouth (OE *gēap*, steep), is reached from the A35 west of Bridport. This steep valley and small bay is very attractive with splendid views east and west along the coast. To the west Thorncombe Beacon (130m) offers especially good vistas. From the top of West Cliff there are lovely views over West Bay to Portland.

West Dorset Council may sell Eype Beach for £1. It was bought by Bridport Town Council in 1932 to prevent gravel extraction. Officials have now decided that there is no reason for the council to continue owning it.

St Peter's Church at Eype has become a venue for many artistic events. Several events take place here every year, ranging from visual art to music. This is but one of the venues in the Bridport area for an arts scene that takes in creative writing, the visual arts, food, design and music.

MV Balmoral at West Bay; built in 1949 and now a Vintage Excursion Ship

The Old Salt Store

Fish & Chips booth

Eype's Mouth Beach and West Cliff

Eype Church Arts Centre

Bluebells in April at Cobey's Castle

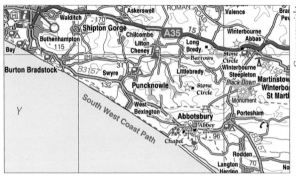

Crown copyright

This area is also very good for migrant birds during spring and autumn. The combination of hedgerows, marshy areas, lagoons and meadows makes it very attractive to birds on passage. The beach is also a good place for seawatches.

Abbotsbury is named for the monastery that was here and the hillfort that overlooks the village from Wears Hill. Abbotsbury Castle is Iron Age and has substantial ramparts which enclose almost 2ha. The view from the B3167 over the village, Chesil Beach and the Fleet (OE *flēot*, inlet) is said to be one of the best in all England.

The village suffered many fires over the centuries and as a result most of the delightful stone buildings date from the 17th and 18th centuries. The huge thatched Tithe Barn is all that remains of the monastery apart from a few walls.

Abbotsbury Swannery was run by the monastery for the production of meat. A large number of Mute Swans are resident here and can be observed at close quarters. Cyg-

Chesil Beach (OE *cisel*, shingle) is a shingle barrier beach which stretches 18mi (29km) from West Bay to Portland. Burton Bradstock (OE *Bride tūn*, River Bride Farm) marks the end of the spectacular sandstone cliffs.

From here the shingle beaches of Burton, Cogden, West Bexington (OE *byxen tūn*, Box tree farm) and Abbotsbury extend in a straight line, backed by small lagoons, and meadows on gentle slopes. Wild flowers abound, with many orchids and other meadow species on the unimproved fields. The beach has species such as Yellow-horned Poppy, Sea Holly, Sea Kale and Thrift.

Burton Cliff from Burton Beach

St Catherine's Chapel by William Daniell in 1822

Yellow-horned Poppy

nets hatch from May onwards. Many other species of waterfowl also breed here.

The Sub-Tropical Gardens were originally established in 1765 by the Countess of Ilchester to supply the castle. They cover 8ha and hold many exotic species. The mix of formal, walled spaces, woodland and less organised parts adds to the interest.

St Catherine's Chapel dates from the 14th century and was part of the monastery. The building is massively constructed completely from local stone on the summit of Chapel Hill (80m), south of the village.

The Fleet is an important wintering area for waterfowl and waders, including Dark Bellied Brent Geese, Egrets, Pochard, Red-breasted Merganser, Coot, Greenshank and Bar-tailed Godwit. In summer Chesil Beach has a breeding colony of Little Terns, which is fenced off to prevent disturbance. Bass and Eels are still caught here, while Oysters are farmed at Ferrybridge.

Abbotsbury from the west with Portland in the background

Abbotsbury Swannery

Abbotsbury Castle is an Iron Age hillfort

Pyramidal Orchid

Abbotsbury houses

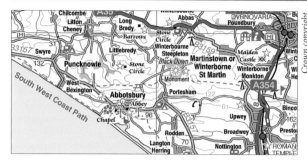

Crown copyright

MEGALITHIC MONUMENTS

The Portesham area has more surviving prehistoric monuments than the rest of Dorset. This is largely due to its geology and position on the Dorset Ridgeway, which has limited the intensity of farming.

The Valley of Stones (SY593873) is a dry chalk valley to the west of Black Down, north of Portesham. This National Nature Reserve has a "Sarsen Boulder Train". These form when sandstone on top

of underlying chalk fractures. Large chunks then slide down the valley sides.

Sarsen stones are a form of sandstone, hardened by silica, which formed above the chalk around 40Mya. During the ice ages these rocks cracked and broke into boulders which proved very useful to Neolithic builders of megalithic monuments.

The Hell Stone (SY604868), on Portesham Hill, is a Ne-

olithic chambered cairn. It was partially "reconstructed" in 1866 when several of the orthostats and a lintel were set up. Originally the cairn was over 20m long and the entrance may have faced the southeast.

The Grey Mare and Her Colts (SY584870, 190m) overlooks Abbotsbury from White Hill. The remains of Dorset's best chambered cairn, this site is a mound about 24m long and 12m wide on the southeast end. Several orthostats and one of the lintels form a confusing heap. The chamber may well have been aligned with the winter solstice sunrise.

Kingston Russell Stone Circle (SY578878, 195m) is on the top of Tenant's Hill, at the intersection of five pathways, about 800m northwest of the Grey Mare. There are fine views over nearby Abbotsbury and to the west. Today all 18 stones lie toppled in an oval about 27 by 18m. This site has an alignment to the winter solstice sunset and perhaps also the summer solstice sunset.

The Nine Stones (SY611903) stand among trees inside a railing fence west of Winterborne Abbas on the busy A35. This is the only remaining intact stone circle in Dorset. Seven of the orthostats are less than 1m high, and form an ellipse about 9m by 8m. The remaining two are nearly 2m high and are on the northwest side. Access is from the Little Chef carpark at Winterborne Abbas.

The Hell Stone

Kingston Russell Stone Circle

The Nine Stones

The Mare and Her Colts

Bronze Age Barrows occur in large numbers all over Dorset. Although many were dug into during the 19th century, the majority remain undisturbed. In the early Bronze Age, burials were mostly single inhumations later, cremation became popular. Most burials were then of ashes within pottery urns or beakers.

The Valley of Stones

The Clandon Barrow (SY656890), north of Maiden Castle, was opened in 1882. It was found to contain an unusually rich array of grave goods, including a large lozenge-shaped gold plate with inscribed lines, as well as a pottery urn, a bronze dagger and an amber incense cup. Some of these can be seen in the museum in Dorchester. A similar intricately designed gold lozenge was found at Bush Barrow near Stonehenge. There has been much speculation about its inscriptions.

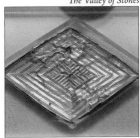

Clandon Barrow gold lozenge

The Hardy Monument

Captain Thomas Hardy

THOMAS MASTERMAN HARDY

The Hardy Monument on Black Down (SY614877, 242m) was built in 1884 to commemorate Vice Admiral Sir Thomas Hardy (1769-1839). It was to him that Nelson said the immortal words, "Kiss me Hardy". He was Flag Captain to Nelson at the Battle of Trafalgar in command of HMS *Victory*. Later, he was First Naval Lord and advocated steam powered warships.

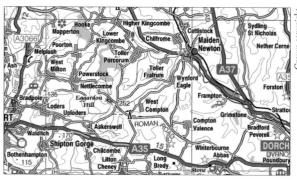

Crown copyright

Common Twayblade

Eggardon Hill (OE *Eohere dūn*, Eohere's Hill SY541947, 252m) is on the side road from Powerstock to Askerswell. It is on the line of the Roman road which runs west out of Dorchester. The hillfort encloses 8ha on a chalk hill.

The principal entrance is to the east, while the southern ramparts have slipped down the hillside and been repaired. Inside there are many depressions, now thought to be storage pits. A large octagonal feature once enclosed a stand of pine trees planted by the famous 17th century smuggler,

Isaac Gulliver who owned the hill. The government felled the wood because it was thought to be involved with the smuggling trade, then rife in Dorset.

The panoramic view from Eggardon Hill is said to be one of the finest in the county. The ramparts are also a haven for wild flowers and butterflies. Orchids, including Common Spotted, Pyramidal, Bee and Fragrant may be seen as well as Autumn Gentian. Butterflies such as Silver-spotted Skippers, Adonis and Chalkhill Blue also breed here.

Roman Road The A35 west from Dorchester follows the Roman road to Exeter for over 3mi (5km). From here a side

road continues all the way to Eggardon Hill. The narrow section west of Compton Valence follows the contours. Parts of the agger can still just be made out in places. From Eggardon Hill the route is unclear but it may well follow the River Asker (or Mangerton) into Bridport, perhaps along a much more ancient trackway.

Powerstock Common (B *power*, OE *stoc*, outlying homestead on the River Power, SY547974, 117ha) is one of the best of the Dorset nature reserves to visit. The abandoned railway line embankments, ancient woodland, marshy areas and varied geology mean that this reserve has an especially diverse range of species.

Roman road west of Dorchester

Eggardon Hill from the southeast showing slumped ramparts

Bee Orchid

Powerstock Common disused railway line and embankments

Wild flower highlights include Bee and Common Spotted Orchid and Common Twayblade. Butterflies include Comma, Marsh and Silver-washed Fritillary, Green Hairstreak and Grizzled Skipper.

Kingcombe Meadows Reserve (DWT, SY553990, 185ha) is a working farm which has never been subject to artificial fertilisers or agrochemicals. Meadows, hedges, streams and woodland are a haven for wildlife, including many wild flowers, butterflies and birds. Perhaps at its best in early summer, it is a step back in time to what farms were like in the early 20th century, before mechanisation, chemicals and intensification.

Compton Valence (OE *cumb tūn*, Valley farm SY595932) is situated north of the A35, 7mi (11km) west of Dorchester. At the head of a narrow chalk valley, it is famous for its plantings of Snowdrops, which form carpets in early spring, followed by Daffodils. During February the village hall serves teas to visitors.

Common Spotted Orchid   *Flower-filled meadow at Kingcombe*

Kingcombe Meadows Nature Reserve

Snowdrops at Compton Valence

CERNE ABBAS & THE CERNE GIANT

Crown copyright

Royal Oak pub, built 1540

CERNE ABBAS (B *cearn-el*, stony, pebbly stream) is on the A352 about 7.5mi (12km) north of Dorchester on the road to Sherborne. The village developed next to the Benedictine Abbey here, founded in AD987. Some parts of the abbey and the 13th century parish church remain.

Many old buildings line the two main streets, some with interesting woodwork. Abbey Street has a line of 16th century houses. The "Royal Oak" is said to be one of the oldest pubs in England. Cerne Abbas was once famous for its beer, which was exported far and wide. The village also supported a variety of cottage industries which all declined in the 19th century.

The Cerne Giant is situated on the west slope of a hill just north of the village. The figure of a naked man with a large erection carrying a ribbed club in his right hand is cut into the hillside. He is 55m high with an 11m penis; the club is 37m long. Recent investigations suggest that there was a cloak or animal skin over the right arm and that there was a severed head on the ground below.

The earliest known illustration of the Cerne Giant was published in the *Gentleman's Magazine* in 1764, although there is a record of it being repaired in 1694. Although there is no evidence of the age of the chalk figure, the most persuasive theory is that he represents Hercules. Whether dating from Roman times or more recently, the Giant has not been without controversy over the years. Being a scheduled ancient monument, his manhood is now protected.

The figure has for long been a fertility symbol. A Maypole was formerly put up on the earthwork above the Giant, where childless couples danced on Mayday. According to folk

Depiction of the Cerne Giant from 1764

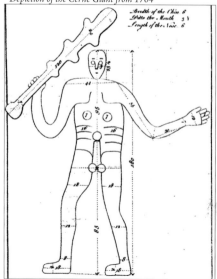

The Cerne Giant from the viewpoint

Abbot's Hall oriel window

Graveyard and Tithe Barn

Abbey Street has many old buildings

belief, a woman who sleeps on the figure will be blessed with fecundity and infertility may be cured through sexual intercourse on top of the figure, especially the phallus.

It is best seen from the air, but there is a good view from a car park off the A352 north of the village. However a much better vantage point is from nearby Weam Common Hill.

Minterne Gardens are about 2mi (3km) north of Cerne Abbas. The gardens were laid out in the style of Capability Brown in the 18th century for the Digby and Churchill families. They are open for much of the year and are especially resplendent from early spring to midsummer. The house is not open to the public.

A Roman depiction of Hercules

14th century doorway in Abbey Street
Minterne House Gardens

St Augustine's Well

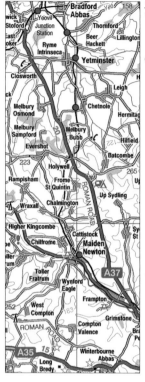

Maiden Newton in former times

Maiden Newton shelters on the east bank of the River Frome at its confluence of the River Hooke, in a gap of the Dorset Downs. It has an old church dating from Norman times. The fire station has one of the oldest operational fire engines in the country.

Lankham Bottom (46ha) and **Hog Cliff Bottom** (87ha) are chalkland nature reserves in small valleys, or combes, which overlook the River Frome. They are famous for their range of downland plants and butterflies. Adonis Blue, Marsh Fritillary, Grizzled and Dingy Skippers may be seen here.

Rampisham Down (OE *hramsa hamm*, Ramsons meadow) is pronounced "Ransom", was the site of a large and very powerful BBC short wave transmitter station from 1940. It was repeatedly bombed by the Germans. The station finally closed in 2011.

Evershot (OE *eofor sciete*, Wild Boar place) nestles in a steep valley west of Holywell off the A37. This pretty little village has a fine street with elevated

Lankham Bottom Nature Reserve

Maiden Newton Church on an old postcard

Hell Corner, near Melbury Bubb

Panoramic view north from Batcombe Hill

The Cross & Hand Stone

pavements and 17th century houses. The Acorn Inn dates from the 16th century and retains much of its character. It has been named as one of the *"Top six Britiush Inns"*.

Cross & Hand (SY632038) is a 1m high oval stone post which may be Saxon. It stands at the roadside overlooking Batcombe, which nestles in a secret little valley. There is an expansive panoramic view over Blackmore Vale from nearby Gore Hill.

Melbury Bubb (OE *mæle burg*, Colourful old ramparts) is a remote little settlement (ST597066) off the A37 near Chetnole. The church of St Mary was probably founded by the Saxons, but has been renovated several times. It is famous for its unique upside down carved font, which maybe be the base of a Saxon cross.

The designs depict animals, including a dog, a stag, a horse and a lion, all with tails tied in mysterious Celtic-style knots. Some have suggested that the carvings are pre-Saxon, just adding to the mystery.

Yetminster (OE *Eata mynster*, Eata's church) is famous for being the birthplace of Benjamin Jesty. In 1774 he inoculated his wife and two sons with pus from a cow infected with cowpox. All survived and soon the scourge of smallpox was controlled by mass vaccinations. He and his wife are buried at Worth Matravers in Purbeck.

The village is situated southwest of Sherborne, away from main roads. It has many attractive 17th century yellow limestone houses. The mid-15th century St Andrew's Church has Part of a Saxon cross on a window ledge, while the base of the font is Norman, suggesting an earlier chapel here.

Saxon cross base reused upside down

The Acorn Inn, Evershot

Melbury Bubb

SHERBORNE

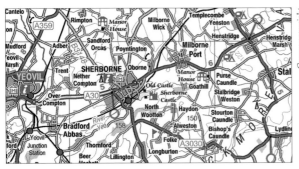

SHERBORNE (OE *scīr burne*, Clear Stream, ST638165, popn. 2011 9,523) is in a fine, south-facing position on a slope above a tributary of the River Yeo. To the southeast is the Blackmore Vale, while Yeovil is 6mi (10km) to the west.

Much of the town is constructed with attractive local ochre ham stone, which lends it a warm, friendly atmosphere. It was the capital of the Saxon kingdom of Wessex. King Alfred the Great was educated at the original Sherborne School. His brothers Kings Ethelbert and Ethelbald were buried in the Abbey.

Sherborne Old Castle, a fortified palace, was built in the early 12th century by Roger de Caen, who was the Chancellor of England as well as the Bishop of Salisbury. Sir Walter Raleigh was given the Sherborne Estate by Elizabeth I in 1592, one of many awards. He initially planned to rebuild the now ruinous Old Castle.

Sherborne (New) Castle Raleigh then built Sherborne Lodge, a rectangular 4-storey house with corner turrets. Finished in 1594, it was to be his summer residence, away from Court in London. After the death of Elizabeth, he was imprisoned in the Tower of London by James I. He was executed in 1618. Meanwhile, James I sold Sherborne Estate to Sir John Digby in 1617.

The Digbys considerably expanded the original Lodge. In the 18th century the grounds were laid out by Lancelot "Capability" Brown. The family still own the estate. The house and gardens are open to the public. Many events are held here each year.

In the Civil War, Sherborne was stoutly Royalist. As a result, the already ruinous Old Castle was largely demolished by Parliamentary forces under General Fairfax in 1645. It is now maintained by English Heritage.

Ruins of Sherborne Old Castle

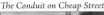

The Conduit on Cheap Street

Sherborne Old Castle

Sherborne New Castle

Walter Raleigh

Shiburnian Alan Turing

Sherborne School opened in 1550, as St Edward's School, a free grammar school for boys. Today it is highly rated and now has around 600 pupils. One of the most illustrious Old Shiburnians is Alan Turing OBE, FRS, the mathematician and computer inventor, who played such a crucial role at Bletchley Park in WWII.

Other interesting old buildings include The Conduit, the Hospice of St Julian and Sherborne House. There is a small museum in the Abbey Almonry, off Cheap Street.

Sherborne Steam and Waterwheel Centre in Oborne Road, near the Old Castle, is based around a 26ft waterwheel dating from 1869. It drives a water pump made in 1883. A Hindley steam engine

similar to that which was also used in the waterworks is also on display along with many other artefacts and documents.

Sherborne has a large selection of independent shops, which will appeal to every taste from high fashion, gourmet foodstuff to books and gifts. There are also many fine places to eat and drink. The march of the franchise outlet, chain store and look-alike restaurant or pub has so far spared this lovely small town.

Sherborne Lake and Gardens

Sherborne has many lovely old buildings

Ochre-coloured ham stone

The nave and choir from the west

Relations between the towns-folk and the monks were not always good. In 1437 a fire-arrow was shot through a window into the nave. At the time wooden scaffolding and a temporary thatched roof were in place due to extensive repairs. The choir and crossing still show fire blackening.

In 1539 John Horsey bought the abbey from the Crown, intending to demolish it and reuse the materials. However, the townspeople managed to buy it for around £66, before it was knocked down, though the lead on the roof cost them another £250. The result was the preservation of a magnificent medieval church. The former people's church of All Hallows was demolished.

SHERBORNE ABBEY was founded in AD705 by the Saxon, King Ine of Wessex who appointed Aldhelm, abbot of Malmesbury, as bishop. There were wenty-six more Saxon bishops and two of their kings buried here in the 9th century. A Saxon doorway and some stonework remain in the northwest corner. In AD998 a Benedictine abbey was established here. The Normans moved the Bishop's See to Old Sarum. No longer a cathedral, the building remained as an abbey church until the Dissolution in 1539.

Many claim that the Abbey, or St Mary's Church, is the finest in Dorset. It certainly includes Saxon, Norman and Medieval features within its complex architecture. The exterior is mostly from rebuilding during the 15th century, with later additions, but close examination will reveal much earlier footings and arches, as well as the fine Norman south porch.

Sherborne Abbey and Close from the southwest

The interior is dominated by the exquisite fan-vaulted roof, which was installed in the late 15th century. The choir roof was completed first, followed by the nave and transepts. The term "fan vaults" arises from the delicate appearance of the stone ribs rising from the pillars, which resemble fans.

Over the centuries the vaults have settled and subsided. To prevent their collapse, parts were rebuilt in the 19th century. During the 20th century, steel beams were mounted in the roof space. Support rods were then bolted to key parts of the vaulting.

The overall ambience inside the church is of space, light and peace. There is a feeling of timelessness as Saxon, Norman and medieval walls, ancient as well as modern windows and a huge variety of woodwork, memorials and decorations blend together. The crossing retains three Norman arches.

Some of the stained glass windows date from the 15th century, but the south and west windows are 19th century. The Great West Window

The Great West Window, 1998 is modern, by the artist John Hayward, and dedicated in 1998 in the presence of HM The Queen and HRH Prince Philip. Other modern touches are the engraved glass reredos by Lawrence Whistler in the ancient Lady Chapel.

St John's Almshouse dates from the 15th century and was expanded in the 19th. The original chapel is very interesting, with a 15th century south window and fine wooden fittings.

The choir

Of greatest note is a 15th century triptych, which may have been painted in Cologne, specifically for this chapel.

St John's Almshouse

Triptych painted in Cologne in the 1400s

St John's Almshouse Chapel

Sherborne Abbey

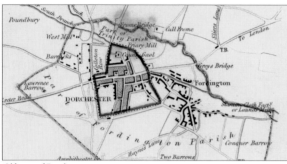

Old map of Dorchester

Roman town wall remnant

DORCHESTER (B *durno*, fist sized stone OE *wara*, people, *ceaster*, walled town, 2011 popn., 19,060) is the county town of Dorset. It is situated on the River Frome in the shadow of the mighty hillfort of Maiden Castle, whose origins date back to the Neolithic.

Neolithic people also built several timber henge monuments, the largest being at Mount Pleasant (SY709899) to the southeast. This was a massive timber circle, 370m in diameter. A smaller version is buried under the Waitrose carpark. Maumbury Rings (OE *malm burh*, chalk earthwork) also dates from these times.

Romans Before the arrival of the Romans in AD43 there may well have been a small

Durotriges settlement above the flood plain of the river Frome. From c.AD70, a new town was built with wooden buildings on a grid plan. The settlement was surrounded by a ditch and bank. Later, in the 3rd century, stone buildings and a defensive town wall were constructed. Maumbury Rings was made into an amphitheatre and many fine houses were built.

Part of the Roman wall remains near the Top of the Town carpark. The footings of a unique Roman Town Touse are behind County Hall. *Durnovaria* was an important regional centre at the intersection of several roads, going east to Wareham, south to Weymouth, west to Exeter, northwest to Ilchester and northeast to Badbury Rings.

A Roman Aqueduct ran 12mi (19km) from the River Frome at Notton, south of Maiden Newton, to Dorchester. It followed the 80m contour with a drop of c.18m along its length. The lade was cut into the chalk and may have been lined with clay with wooden sides and top to prevent water loss. The aqueduct seems to have been abandoned by c.AD160.

Remains of the earthworks and channel can be seen at several places along the Roman road west of the River Frome heading northeast from Dorchester towards Bradford Peverell. There are good sections at Poundbury hillfort and from there towards the A37 bypass. The aqueduct would have supplied the Roman fort and the town of *Durnovaria*.

Poundbury hillfort and Roman aqueduct

Roman aqueduct near Bradford Peverell

Roman town house behind County Hall

THE ORIGIN OF THE NAME "DORCHESTER"

Although Dorset is mentioned in the *Anglo-Saxon Chronicle* in AD891, the root is very much older. Many variations occur, but all include the prefix dorn, (B *durno-*, large round pebble or fist). Quite probably the name derives from the pebbles deposited by the rivers. The Romans called Dorchester *Durnovaria*, most likely from the original local name, and probably pronounced as *Dornawara* by the locals. Later, the Saxons added a suffix (OE *ceaster*, walled town) to give *Dornwaraceaster*, soon shortened to Dorchester.

Saxons & Normans During Saxon times, Dorchester developed into a centre for textile weaving and trading. By 1066 there were 153 houses here. The town thrived along the axis of the Roman road and within the old Roman walls. A Norman castle stood on the site of the prison, now closed.

Early Tourist In c.1725 Daniel Defoe wrote in *"A tour thro'* the Whole Island of Great Britain"; "The town is populous, tho' not large, the streets broad, but the buildings old, and low; however, there is good company and a good deal of it; and a man that coveted a retreat in this world might as agreeably spend his time, and as well in Dorchester, as in any town I know in England".

Fires Much of the town was burnt in fires in 1613 and

DORCHESTER	
Athelhampton	66
Bloody Assizes	57
Cider Museum	67
County Museum	56
Dinosaur Museum	59
Grey's Bridge	61
Hangman's Cottage	58
Higher Bockhampton	62
Keep Military Museum	57
Kingston Maurward	66
Maiden Castle	64
Maumbury Rings	54
Max Gate	62
Napper's Mite	60
Old Courthouse	56
Poundbury	61
Poundbury Hillfort	54
Puddletown Forest	66
RAF Warmwell	67
Roman Aqueduct	54
Roman Roads	66
Roman Townhouse	54
St Peter's Church	56
Teddy Bear Museum	59
Terracotta Warriors	59
Thomas Hardy	62
Thorncombe Wood	66
Tolpuddle Martyrs	68
Town Walks	56
Tutankhamen Exhibition	59
Whitcombe Church	65

Roman mosaic in the County Museum

Maumbury Rings - a Neolithic henge, used by the Romans as an amphitheatre

High West Street around 1900

the town. It dates from the 15th century and despite 19th century renovations, it retains much of its ancient charm. A 16 year old Thomas Hardy was involved in drawing the plans as he was apprenticed to the architect John Hicks at the time.

Dorset County Museum was built in 1883. It is owned and managed by the Dorset Natural History and Archaeological Society. The first curator was the highly effective Henry Joseph Moule (1825-1904).

Today the Museum houses extensive collections covering Jurassic, Ancient, Rural and Writers' Dorset. There are also Victorian and Dorchester galleries. The geology section has many Jurassic Coast fossils. The extensive archaeology displays include interesting artefacts from Maiden Castle and Roman Dorchester.

Shire Hall was built in 1797 and houses the 19th century Crown Court. It was here that the Tolpuddle Martyrs were tried and sentenced to transportation by a somewhat hysterical establishment. The building belongs to the TUC,

1725, leaving only the Antelope Hotel and a Tudor Almshouse from medieval times. As a result much of the town was rebuilt in Georgian style. It remained small until the late 19th century, when development picked up due to the enclosure of adjacent Duchy of Cornwall land in 1874. This created space for expansion, just as Poundbury has in recent times.

The Town Walks are a good place to start a visit to Dorchester. These follow the line of the old Roman town defences and were built in the 18th century before the town expanded. A small section of Roman wall remains near the Top of the Town car park, which is a good place to leave the car and admire a fine statue of Thomas Hardy.

Like many towns with an extensive history, Dorchester has one long street running west to east, High West Street and High East Street, with South Street at right angles. They derive from the Roman road that once ran through the town. All of the main attractions are contained within a small area.

Streets The High Street has changed little since the 1860s or earlier. It is lined with many 18th and 19th century buildings which today house shops, restaurants, pubs, hotels, offices, museums and even houses. The lack of modern developments gives the centre of Dorchester a coherent, genuine appearance.

St Peter's Church is one of very few medieval buildings in

St Peter's Church dates from the 15th century

Keep Military Museum

Dorset County Museum in the 1880s

which has preserved the court room and cells as they were in the early 19th century. It is open to visitors in the summer.

The Antelope Hotel dates from the 17th century and is infamous as one of the venues for the "Bloody Assizes" held after the failed Monmouth Rebellion of 1685. It is now a restaurant, but retains many original features.

The Keep Military Museum is housed near the Top of the Town roundabout in the prominent remains of an old barracks. The Keep dates from 1879 when the new Dorchester Depot Barracks were opened. It is the last remnant of barracks first established here in 1805.

The impressive Dorchester Brigade Depot is a somewhat ponderous building. The ground floor consisted of prisoners' cells, a guard room and exercise yard. The upper stories were used as storage for weapons, munitions and other military supplies.

The museum tells the story of the Devon and Dorset Regiments from beginnings in 1685 to the present day. The awarding of battle honours started in the 18th century and continues to this day. The many campaigns in which the Devons and Dorsets have seen action in over 300 years are covered in the displays. There are panoramic views from the battlements on a clear day.

THE "BLOODY ASSIZES"

The failed Monmouth Rebellion of 1685 led to the "Bloody Assizes", show trials presided over by Lord Chief Justice George Jeffries. Over 1,400 people were tried, the majority being sentenced to death for high treason, for which the penalty was to be hanged, disembowelled and butchered.

Only about 300 were actually executed, while over 800 were sold as slaves in the West Indies, some were released and the rest died of Typhus in gaol. At least one woman was burnt alive. In Dorset the gruesome sentences were carried out in Dorchester, Lyme Regis, Bridport, Weymouth, Wareham, Poole and Sherborne.

Jeffries became known as the "hanging judge", but he could have argued that he was merely carrying out the law of the time. Actually it was King James II himself who was behind the brutal reprisals against those who dared to try to usurp his position.

Within a year a famous secret meeting was held at Charborough House which led to the Glorious Revolution of 1688. Henceforth the monarchy was answerable to Parliament, the rule of law was supreme, and the stage was set for the Enlightenment and the Industrial Revolution.

The Antelope Hotel from an old postcard

The Penfold pillar box from the 1860s

One of the Chideock Martyrs

Terracotta Warrior

Unusual Mailbox Where South Street meets South Walks there is a hexagonal Victorian mailbox on the corner. This type of pillar box was designed by architect John Penfold in 1866 and became known as the Penfold box. These post boxes came in nine variants and were exported to India, Australia, New Zealand and even Uruguay, but not Scotland.

There are several other interesting old postboxes in Dorset. These include the oldest pillar box in the UK at Barnes Cross, south of Sherborne, which dates from 1853. There is an even older wooden postbox in Combe Street, Lyme Regis.

The Dorset Martyrs were some of hundreds of people executed for being practising Catholics in England in the 16th and 17th centuries. Most were found guilty of high treason, the penalty for which was to be hung, then castrated, drawn and quartered while still conscious. The body parts were then displayed prominently in public places as a strong anti-Catholic message.

The Gallows were on the corner of Icen Way and South Walks, where three poignant statues by Elizabeth Frink stand today. They commemorate the victims of sectarian state sponsored murder. In c.1703 the gallows were moved to Maumbury Rings, where executions were watched by thousands of people.

Hangman's Cottage is a pretty thatched building beside the

The Chideock Martyrs

Maumbury Rings in the 1700s

Hangman's Cottage and Frome footpath

diverted southern loop of the River Frome. This was the Millstream which powered a number of watermills in former times. A footpath follows its course around the north of the town, crossing several small bridges along the way.

Small Museums Dorchester is also home to a number of eclectic family-orientated mini museums, all situated off the High Street. Adult visitors will either love them or hate them, but in reality most are aimed at children, who generally are enthralled by them.

The Dinosaur Museum in Icen Way is a family-orientated hands-on experience. The displays are firmly aimed at dinosaur-obsessed children rather than their parents. There are full sized models, dinosaur bones, fossils and interactive computer displays. Touching of the exhibits is encouraged in contrast to most museums.

The Tutankhamen Exhibition *"features the major treasures meticulously recreated, wherever possible, in their original materials... in addition, the ante-chamber and burial cham-*

Christmas lights

ber Tutankhamen's tomb have been accurately recreated together with all the tomb furniture and treasures.."

The Terracotta Warriors Museum *"features a small but spectacular group of these warriors, which have been specially replicated by museum and conservation technicians in China. Also featured are fabulous costumed recreations of the First Emperor of China, Qin Shih Huang di, himself and his uniformed officers."*

The Teddy Bear Museum *"has Edward Bear and his family of people-sized bears, in Teddy Bear House. From the earliest antique teddy bears to today's TV favourites they are all waiting to greet you in this enchanting museum."*

Tutankhamen Exhibition

Dinosaur Museum

Teddy Bear Museum

Grey's Bridge over the River Frome

Dorchester has succeeded in retaining its identity and character due to its small size, geographical position, lack of motorways and rural outlooks. Although there are supermarkets and chain stores, the High Street and main shopping areas are still dominated by independent outlets. The town features a diverse range of restaurants and food shops, as well as easy parking.

Pedestrian Precinct Most of South Street is pedestrian only, which adds greatly to the centre of the town. The many small lanes are home to interesting shops and other businesses. Though not traffic free, they are a delight to explore.

The Borough Gardens between Cornwall Road and West Walks were opened in the 1890s. Later, a bandstand was added. Poundbury hillfort

had already been enclosed in 1876 and declared to be for "public enjoyment" in 1876. It was saved from destruction in the 1850s when the railway company was forced to dig a tunnel rather than an immense cutting for the Dorchester to Yeovil main line.

Train Stations Dorchester still has two railway stations. The Southampton and Dorchester Railway arrived in 1847 and was originally planned to continue to Exeter. The Great Western Railway built another station in 1857. The companies operated joint services to Weymouth, which required complex shunting. Dorchester South Station is set to be the first solar-powered train station in the UK.

Napper's Mite Almshouse in South Street is one of a very few old buildings to survive the fire of 1725 that ravaged most of the town. It was built in 1616 for Sir Robert Napper to accommodate ten old men. It has many original features despite a major renovation in 1842. Today it is a restaurant and coffee shop.

Napper's Mite Almshouse was founded in 1615 to house "ten aged men"

The River Frome floodplain

The Borough Gardens in c.1900

Poundbury from the west

Grey's Bridge was built c.1748 across the River Frome on the eastern side of the town. Mrs Pitt (née Grey) from nearby Kingston Maurward House paid £1,500 to build the new bridge and causeway across the floodplain, nearly in line with the Roman route. Today it is still the main northeast route from the A35.

Dorchester is at the heart of the Dorset road system just as in Roman times when their roads went out north, south, east and west. Journeys through the county inevitably seem to traverse its convenient bypass. The town may be small in comparison to others, but it has much to offer the visitor whether shopping, culture, fossils, Roman artefacts or simply to try its restaurants.

Poundbury from the north

Dorset Museum

Antelope Walk

The Corn Exchange

POUNDBURY

Part of the Duchy of Cornwall, Poundbury has been under development since 1993. This "urban village" has been designed with much input from HRH Prince Charles, who, as the Prince of Wales, owns the Duchy. The Luxembourgian architect, Leon Kreir was responsible for the overall concept.

Opinions vary about this large, brick-built new town, but the development is both different and highly impressive. Plans include 2,500 houses and apartments as well as shops, offices and major services, including Dorset Fire and Rescue Service HQ.

Poundbury was planned in *New Urbanist* style which aims to discourage use of cars in favour of walking, cycling and buses. The designs are a mixture of European, neo-classical and British. Most of the buildings are built with bricks, but in a very different style compared to Dorchester.

THOMAS HARDY & DORCHESTER

Thomas Hardy statue in Dorchester by Eric Kennington (1932)

THOMAS HARDY was born in 1840 in a cob and thatch cottage in Higher Bockhampton (SY728925) which was built by his grandfather. The cottage is now owned by the National Trust. It is next to Thorncombe Woods nature reserve, with its well preserved section of Roman road.

He designed the house at Max Gate, situated just east of the town off the A35 bypass road. Hardy lived and worked here from 1885 until his death. Today the house belongs to the National Trust. It retains some of his furniture but, ultimately, it is now a rather empty place.

During the construction of the house and over a century later with the A35 bypass in 1987, a 100m diameter Neolithic enclosure was destroyed. Just to the east another immense Neolithic henge monument at Mount Pleasant is also hardly visible.

The Dorset Museum housess Thomas Hardy's Study, as the Museum says, *"A Writers' Dorset contains a reconstruction of Thomas Hardy's third study from his home at Max Gate, where he wrote The Dynasts and many poems. All the furniture, books and personal possessions in the room originally belonged to Hardy. On Hardy's desk under the window can be seen the pens which he used to write Tess of the D'Urbervilles and Jude the Obscure, and a perpetual calendar set at the date of his first meeting with his first wife, Emma Gifford."*

Hardy's heart is buried beside his first wife, Emma Gifford, in Stinsford cemetery, off the A35 near Higher Bockhampton. His ashes were buried in Poets' Corner in Westminster Abbey next to those of Charles Dickens. According to the abbey website, *"his chief mourners were his widow, his sister, the Prime Minister Ramsay MacDonald, Rudyard Kipling, Sir James Barrie, George Bernard Shaw and A.E. Housman."*

Thomas Hardy's novels are all set in southwest England, which he called "Wessex" according to its Saxon name. He took many real places, but renamed them, using them as he said, "as a merely realistic dream country." His "Wessex" started with the Dorchester area but in his later novels included Wiltshire, Hampshire, Berkshire, Oxford and Somerset.

His use of the places, people and his romantic yet fateful descriptions still draw visitors today. His literary construct of "Wessex" resonates to many today just as much as in his lifetime and helps make southwest England a strong draw to people.

Hardy met his first wife, Emma Gifford, in 1870 when he was in Cornwall on a restoration project at St Juliot parish church. They were married in 1874 but had no family. Later, they lived apart in Max Gate. He was much affected by her death in 1912, which caused an outpouring of poetry.

He then married Florence Dugdale, his long time secretary, in

Max Gate where Hardy lived from 1885-1927

Hardy's study in Dorchester Museum

Hardy's Cottage interior

Thomas Hardy's birthplace at Higher Bockhampton

1914. She was 39 years younger, and, devoted to Hardy, compiled *"The Early Life of Thomas Hardy 1841-1891"* soon after his death.

Hardy was awarded the Order of Merit in 1910 and received many people at Max Gate as he became more and more famous. He was particularly respected and admired by the next generation of authors such as DH Lawrence, JC Powys, Virginia Woolf and Robert Graves.

Thomas Hardy's Wessex (1902)

Emma Gifford

Thomas Hardy in later life

Florence Dugdale

Gravestone, Stinsford

Stinsford Church graveyard

HERE·LIES·THE·HEART·OF
THOMAS HARDY·O·M
SON·OF·THOMAS·AND·JEMIMA·HARDY

WAS·BORN·AT·UPPER·BOCKHAMPTON·2·JUNE
·DIED·AT·MAX·GATE·DORCHESTER·11·JANUARY
ASHES·REST·IN·POETS·CORNER·WESTMINSTER·A

Maiden Castle

Aerial view of Maiden Castle taken in 1935

Maiden Castle (B *mai dūn*, big hill SY669884, 132m, 19ha) is easily the most impressive of over 30 hillforts in Dorset. Over 1,400 such defensive structures are known in England and Wales, but Maiden Castle was the first one to be extensively excavated. It is situated about 1.5mi (2km) southwest of Dorchester.

During the 1930s, Mortimer Wheeler carried out extensive excavations here. In the 1980s, Niall Sharples did further work, which allowed radioactive dating. Despite its importance, the site was only made a Scheduled Ancient Monument in 1997 and is now looked after by English Heritage.

During the Neolithic Age, around 4000BC, an oval causewayed enclosure was built on the east end of the hill. Two ditches and a bank surrounded an area of about 10 acres. After being abandoned in c.3,400BC, a huge bank barrow was built here. This was 550m long, with ditches on each side, 20m apart. There was no evidence for any burials at this time.

In the Bronze Age, about 1800BC, the hilltop was cultivated for a time then abandoned until the Iron Age. In c.600AD, the first hillfort here covered about 6ha and was enclosed by a ditch with an 8m high rampart. There

were entrances at both the east and west ends. The site was most likely inhabited by a large number of families.

In c.450AD, Maiden Castle was developed into the largest hillfort in Britain. It covered 19ha (47 acres) and was surrounded by a ditch and rampart. Later, the ditch also enclosed adjacent Hog Hill and the rampart heightened to 3.5m. On the south side four ramparts and three ditches were dug, but only three to the steep-sided north.

Square structures about 2m across, which may have been for grain storage, were present. The bases of large numbers of roundhouses built in rows suggest that the ramparts enclosed a large village. There was evidence of bronze working but not of iron smelting. Later, most of the pottery was imported from the Poole area.

By 100BC the settlement was in decline but there was substantial iron working being done. Excavation of an extensive cemetery in the eastern gateway de-

The western defences of Maiden Castle

fences revealed at least 14 skeletons which showed evidence of violent deaths. One has a Roman ballista bolt lodged in his spine. Whether this was sustained during a Roman attack is not clear.

The hillfort remained partially in use until c.100AD and many Roman artefacts have been found, suggesting that they may have used part of the site for military purposes for a time. Maiden Castle was abandoned as *Durnovaria* developed into the civitas of the *Durotriges*, later to become Dorchester.

In c.370AD a Romano-British temple was constructed at the

The western gateway has complex defences

east end of Maiden Castle. It had a room about 6m square with a 3m wide surrounding enclosure. A small house and possible shrine were also built and the eastern entrance to the fort was repaired. After this the site was abandoned.

Slingshot ammunition

Archaeologist excavating skeletons

Roman weapons

Mithras figure from temple

Skeleton with ballista bolt in spine

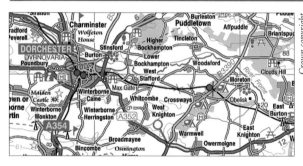

...ston Maurward College. The formal gardens cover 13ha in 18ᵗʰ century Capability Brown style. A lake, canals and sweeping lawns complete the scene.

The Animal Park is a favourite for children, with rare breeds of Dorset sheep, as well as cows, goats, horses, chickens and other animals. Outdoor adventure days for teenagers allow participants to experience how animals are looked after, fed and mucked out.

Athelhampton House is a 15ᵗʰ century manor house first built in the 1490s. The interior roof of the Great Hall is original and spectacular. Its formal gardens cover 8ha and are enclosed in a loop of the River Piddle. They were designed by Inigo Jones in the 1890s and are considered to be one of the greatest of their genre in England.

The visitor centre has the Topiary restaurant and an interesting shop. Althelhampton is open all year with visiting times available on its website. The house is signposted off the A35, east of Puddletown, 5mi (8km) from Dorchester.

The Roman Road from Badbury Rings to Dorchester passes through Puddletown Forest. It can be followed for over 1.5mi (2km) eastwards through Thorncombe Wood, over Bhompston Heath and then via Puddletown Forest to a side road. It continues east through Ilsington Wood.

The woods have a wide range of trees as well as extensive heathland and a small pond. Birds include Dartford War-blers, Nightjars and Woodpeckers. Adders, Grass Snakes and Common Lizards may be seen as well as dragonflies. Park at the Hardy's Cottage carpark or at SY744925 on the side road.

Kingston Maurward House is a large Georgian mansion built in c.1720 by George Pitt. The house and grounds are just east of Dorchester off the A35. They belong to Dorset County Council and are used by King-

Roman Road in Thorncombe Wood

Roman Aqueduct to Durnovaria

Kingston Maurward House

Athelhampton House

Owermoigne Cider Museum

Whitcombe (SY717883), on the A352 1,5mi (2km) southeast of Dorchester, has a delightful small 12th century church. This was the first charge of the minister, poet and philologist, William Barnes (1801-1886). 10th century Saxon carved stones and 14th century frescoes, including of St Christopher, make this lovely little church a real gem.

RAF Warmwell was a fighter station throughout WWII, having been established in 1937. During the Battle of Britain two Spitfire squadrons were based here. Later, in 1944, RAF *Typhoons*, USAAF *P-38 Lightnings*, *P-47 Thunderbolts* and other aircraft operated from here. They undertook intensive ground attack missions before, during and after D-Day all over northern France.

The modern village of Crossways now covers much of the former airfield. A memorial to those who served here in WWII is situated near the site of the operations room. Little remains of the base except for two Bellman hangars and a few derelict buildings.

Cider Museum (SY773870) is 1.5mi (2km) north of Owermoigne off the A352. It displays presses, apple mills and other cider making equipment from the 18th and 19th centuries. The transition from home-made timber equipment to presses and crushers using cast iron components is well told. Locally made ciders can be tasted and purchased here. The Mill House Nurseries here are very tempting to all gardeners with their huge range of seed potatoes, tomato plants and other vegetables.

Flowers and fruit trees are also available in profusion.

Heathland Nature Reserves Tadnoll (SY792873, 44ha) and Winfrith Heath (SY805870, 103ha) have a great variety of wildlife. Dry and wet heath together with acid bogs and pools attract typical heathland birds and insects. The marshy areas support the rare Marsh Gentian as well as the insectivorous Pale Butterwort and two species of sundew.

Whitcombe Church

Tadnoll Heath Nature Reserve

Aircrew and Hawker Tempest at RAF Warmwell

The Tolpuddle Martyrs

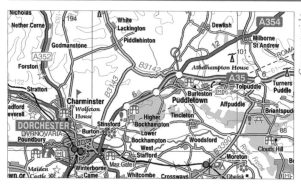

The jury found the defendants guilty of seditious oath taking and they were handed down the maximum sentence, which was seven year's transportation to Australia. Essentially the men had been framed under a law intended to quell mutiny in the Royal Navy because trade unions were seen as a threat to the vested interests of the landed gentry.

The Tolpuddle Martyrs were six farm workers who formed the "Friendly Society of Agricultural Labourers" in Tolpuddle in 1833. The Combination Acts which made workers combining together to seek better wages and conditions illegal, were repealed in the 1820s. Further, the Reform Act of 1832 had paved the way for eventual democracy.

After the end of the Napoleonic and American Wars in 1815, the huge demand for supplies by Royal Navy and Army soon disappeared. This created a recession in agriculture. At the same time mechanisation and modernisation was driving down the requirement for large numbers of farm labourers and thus their wages also.

The group was led by **George Loveless**, who was a Methodist preacher. They met in Thomas Standfield's house, where they swore an oath of secrecy together. Although trade unions were now explicitly legal, charges were brought under a 1797 law designed to prevent seditious meetings.

The trial was held in Dorchester Assizes in March 1834, presided over by Judge Baron Williams. The Jury was packed with the local MP, as well as magistrates and land owners. The judge stated at the outset that, *"The object of all legal punishment is not altogether with the view of operating on the offenders themselves, it is also for the sake of offering an example and a warning,"*

The "convicts" were duly sent to Australia aboard transport ships where the conditions were very bad. Loveless stated, *"To enumerate the various miseries and evils which prisoners are subjected to from the time of landing in the colony until their death, would be utterly impossible; suffice it to say it is dreadful in the extreme, so much so that a person who has never been there can have no idea of it."*

Within days a Grand Meeting of the Working Classes was attended by over 10,000 participants. On 21st April 1834 about 100,000 people processed through Copenhagen Fields near King's Cross in London. The protest was led by Robert Owen, the founder of the Co-operative Movement, and marched to Whitehall under strict discipline. The streets were lined by cheering crowds.

The Home Secretary, Lord Melbourne, who had supported the trial, refused to come out and take the petition presented. The government, fearful of trouble had gone

The Martyrs' Tree, Tolpuddle

JAMES BRINE   THOMAS STANFIELD   JOHN STANFIELD   GEORGE LOVELESS   JAMES LOVELESS

completely over the top, having drafted in cavalry, infantry and cannon. Luckily they were not foolish enough to try to use the military against the protest.

Pressure from MPs, petitions with over 800,000 signatories and popular pressure finally forced action. The new Home Secretary, John Russell, granted conditional pardons in June 1835. Eventually, in March 1836, after many more petitions to Parliament, the men were fully pardoned.

Although one of the men returned to work in Dorset all of the rest ended up in London, Ontario. James Loveless wrote a pamphlet called "The Vic-

tims of Whiggery", which was used by the growing Chartists' Movement, which advocated, 'The People's Charter': Manhood Suffrage, Voting by secret ballot, Payment of MPs, Annual Parliaments, Abolition of property qualifications for MPs Equal electoral districts.

Today the events of 1833-1836 are seen as early successes in the birth of the trade unions. Eventually workers were to succeed in gaining better terms and conditions and the balance between employers and employees became less polarised and fairer.

The Tolpuddle Martyrs Museum "tells the harrowing tale

The Tolpuddle Martyrs' in a contemporary drawing of the Martyrs' arrest, trial and punishment, leading to the foundation of modern day trade unionism."

Tolpuddle remains a place of pilgrimage for trade unionists, but it should also be seen as a symbol of a desire for fairness and democracy.

Tolpuddle Martyrs' Memorial

The Authorities' Warning

Copenhagen Fields protest April 1834

Chesil Beach from Portland Heights

The Jubilee Clock

WEYMOUTH (B *Wey* OE *mũða*, Mouth of the River Wey, popn. 52,323 in 2011) is today an attractive holiday resort town. Its beautiful wide sandy beach extends for 2.2mi (3.5km) all around east-facing Weymouth Bay.

Melcombe Regis (OE *melce cumb*, milk producing valley) is the oldest part of the town, and is clustered around the harbour on the north side of the river. It was a significant deep water port during the Iron Age. The Romans developed the harbour to supply their military and the town of *Durnovaria*, now Dorchester.

The A354 follows the Roman road to Dorchester. Remains of villas, harbour works and warehouses have been discovered, but the only Roman ruin visible is a small temple at Jordan Hill (SY698812) where many artefacts and a cemetery have been found nearby.

Early Military History The first major military developments in Weymouth were the Roman harbour, wharves and temporary fort originating in AD43. By c.AD70 Dorset was peaceful and became a prosperous part of Roman Britain.

In 1537, Henry VIII commenced building the "Device Forts". These were a series of coast defences which ran from Cornwall to Northumberland. The Dissolution of the Monasteries Act, 1536, and subsequent rift with Rome, meant that there was an imminent risk of war with France or Spain.

Viking War Cemetery In 2009, during the construction of a new section of main road on Ridgeway Hill, the grizzly remains of 51 Viking warriors were discovered. They had all been killed, decapitated and dismembered during the late 10th century, perhaps in an abortive raid.

Melcombe has the dubious record of probably being the port through which bubonic plague arrived in Britain in 1348. It was spread by Black Rats carrying fleas infected with a particularly virulent strain of *Yersinia pestis* bacterium. The devastating result was at least a third of the population dead.

By the 16th century, Weymouth had developed on the southern side of the harbour. The

Weymouth in 1822 by William Daniell

The Esplanade from the south end of the Beach

two towns were amalgamated in 1571, and the first Town Bridge was built in 1594. This was by now a very busy port, depending on the Newfoundland Grand Banks codfish trade. Salt fish was exported to the West Indies and Portugal. Return cargoes were of Caribbean sugar and rum, or Portuguese wine and port.

Emigrants Weymouth was one of the first ports of embarkation for Massachusetts. The Reverend John White of Dorchester was instrumental in organising these early voyages. The first was the *Abigail* in 1625, followed by John Endicott on the *Amity* in 1628.

From 1787, Weymouth was one of the ports of departure of ships "transporting" criminals to Botany Bay, Tasmania and other places in Australia. This had actually started in the 1620s when America and the West Indies were the convicts' final destinations.

The town was staunchly Parliamentarian in the Civil War. In 1642 it withstood a 19-day siege by the Royalists. The devastation and disruption greatly reduced trade in the town, which was soon overtaken as a port by Poole.

Early Tourism Weymouth's sheltered position, mild cli-

WEYMOUTH	
Bennett's Water Gardens	78
Burning Cliff	79
Chesil Beach	76, 78
East Fleet	76
Emigration	73
Esplanade	74
Ferry Bridge	76
Fleet	78
George III Statue	74
Jubilee Clock	74
Lodmoor Country Park	77
Mail Packets	76
Melcombe Regis	72
Moonfleet	78
Nature Reserves	77
Osmington White Horse	79
Pleasure Pier	76
Radipole Lake	77
Ringstead Bay	79
Rodwell Trail	76
Roman Temple	72
Sand Sculptures	74
Sandsfoot Castle	76
Sea Life Park	78
Sea Life Tower	76
Shopping Precinct	75
Smuggler's Path	79
South Pier	76
The Nothe Fort	80
Tudor House	75
Upwey Wishing Well	74
Viking War Cemetery	72
Weymouth Bay	72
Weymouth Harbour	75
White Nothe	79
Wyke Regis	76

Old postcard view of the beach and Esplanade

The north side of the Old Harbour

mate and proximity to London made it very attractive to rich Georgians in the late 18th century. The fashion for taking the waters in spas and sea bathing suddenly became popular, greatly encouraged by the medical profession. Soon the Royal Family took an interest. First the Duke of Gloucester, younger brother of King George III, then the King himself became fans. The King and his family stayed here nearly every summer from 1789 to 1805.

Upwey Wishing Well, north of the town (SY660853), had been popular for years and George III had a special gold cup made to partake of its waters. However it was the sulphurous springs at Nottington and Radipole that really drew the people wishing to benefit from the spa waters.

Esplanade The beautiful curved Georgian and Regency terraces of the Esplanade were built between the 1780s and

1850s. Rich businessmen commissioned famous architects to flaunt their wealth. Today many are hotels or guest houses with shops and offices on the ground floor at the southern end.

In preparation for the sailing events of the 2012 Olympic Games, Weymouth was given an extensive refurbishment. Both the 1887 Jubilee Clock, which celebrates the 50th year of Queen Victoria's reign, and the King George III statue, were repaired and repainted.

Sand Sculptures have been a feature of Weymouth for over 90 years, initially by Fred Darrington and continued by his grandson, Mark Anderson. Many famous landmarks, objects and characters have featured among the impressive creations here. The

Upwey Well

Pedestrian area

King George III statue

One of many Fish and Chips outlets

Sand sculpture

Weymouth sand is especially well-suited to this form of art.

Trinity Street, off Hope Square on the south side of the harbour, has some of the oldest houses in town. The 17th century Tudor House Museum has mullioned windows and contemporary furnishings. Nearby, a 16th century merchant's house, the Old Rooms, became the town's first assembly rooms in the 18th century.

Shopping Precinct Behind the Esplanade there are several small streets, some of which are pedestrianised. Apart from the ubiquitous chain stores, there are many and varied independent shops stocking a huge variety of goods. Being a seaside resort, Weymouth also has its fair share of retailers selling all manner of more traditional things to visitors, ranging from souvenirs to angling equipment and scuba gear.

Weymouth Harbour is comparatively deep and sheltered. It is still one of the largest fishing ports in England and the outer end is a working port, handling ferries and freighters. The inner harbour is now a

The Old Harbour from the Town Bridge

The Old Rooms

Pulteney Buildings

Customs House

The beach amusements

The Old Harbour

large marina. Sea angling, diving and sight-seeing trips are all run from here.

The quaysides of the Old Harbour have many interesting buildings. These include the blue-painted no 2 Trinity Road, holiday home of a Robert Allen from Bath. He was an early proponent of bathing in the sea here. This street has numerous other fine colourful houses to admire.

The north side of the Old Harbour is lined with redundant warehouses, now hotels, apartments, pubs and restaurants. Heavy bombing during WWII, followed by postwar demolition, destroyed much of the old centre of Weymouth.

Weymouth Sea Life Tower, on the end of the Pleasure Pier, was opened in 2012. Its viewing capsule rotates slowly as it rises to 53m above sea level, offering a dramatic panoramic view of the surrounding area. It belongs to Merlin Entertainments of Poole, who also run the Sea Life Park at Lodmoor.

Mail Packets and Ferries In 1794, Weymouth was chosen by the Royal Mail as the port for its new packet service to the Channel Islands. By 1827 the first steamships were operating from here, while the railway arrived in 1857. From 1993 to early 2015, Condor Ferries ran fast catamaran ferries from Weymouth but they all now depart from Poole.

Wyke Regis (OE *wíc*, harbour, bay) forms the southern suburbs of Weymouth. The Rodwell Trail follows the line of the former Great Western railway line from central Weymouth to Ferry Bridge. This 2mi (3km) walkers' and cyclists' path passes Sandsfoot Castle and Gardens along the way. There are fine views over Portland Harbour and Portland from the south end.

Ferry Bridge crosses the narrow estuary of The Fleet to Chesil Beach. Before the first bridge was built in 1839 a small ferry made the crossing. This was treacherous in bad weather. The present bridge dates from 1985.

The Fine Foundation Chesil Beach Centre is run by Dorset Wildlife Trust. Displays here explain the geology and ecology of Chesil Beach and the lagoon behind it, The Fleet. The Fleet Observer runs daily boat trips in the summer.

Sandsfoot Castle (SY675773) was built in 1541 as a protected emplacement for cannon. The magazines were in the

The 2012 Olympic Games sailing events were held at Weymouth

Sea Life Tower

basement and there was accommodation for about 50 soldiers. It was surrounded by a ditch and rampart, now part of the gardens.

It was already ruinous by 1584, but repaired in the early 1600s. The Royalists held it during the Civil War but abandoned it as of no value in 1645. It was out of use by 1690 and subsequently became a convenient quarry. In view of the fact that much of the stone may have come from Bindon Abbey near Wool this seems a fitting end.

Situated just off the Rodwell Trail, Sandsfoot Castle is today a gaunt ruin set in attractive gardens. It has been stabilised and provided with walkways for safe access.

Nature Reserves Weymouth has two wetland RSPB reserves, both within the town. **Radipole Lake** (OE *hrēodiy pōl*, Reedy Pool) covers 78ha of the Wey estuary, separated from the sea by a dam. It comprises a freshwater lake, reed beds, shallow ponds and a former saltmarsh. The Wild Weymouth Discovery Centre is next to the Swannery carpark.

There are two nature trails complete with viewing points and hides. The reserve is excellent for birds all year round. Reed, Sedge, Grasshopper and Cetti's Warblers as well as Bearded Tits all breed here. In summer Hobbys may be seen hawking for dragonflies. The

Sandsfoot Castle dates from the time of Henry VIII

many wild flowers make it a good place to seek butterflies. In winter large numbers of wildfowl congregate here, while muddy areas attract waders such as Dunlin, Redshank and Snipe.

Bittern overwinter among the reeds, the booming calls being heard near twilight. Well camouflaged, they are difficult to spot except when they arrive to roost or move to feed.

Lodmoor RSPB Reserve (B *lūta* OE *mōr*, Muddy Moor) is signposted off the A353, northeast of the Sea Life Park. Covering 61ha, this area has brackish pools, saltmarsh, marshy grass and bushes. There is a nature trail and three hides.

Similar species may be seen as at Radipole Lake. Bearded Tits and Cetti's Warblers are resident, while the reserve

Bearded Tit

Chiffchaff

Radipole Lake

Bennett's Water Gardens

small village of Fleet surrounds the new church built in 1829. A particularly violent storm, in 1824, demolished much of the old church near the sea.

The village is the setting of the very successful novel *Moonfleet*, by J Meade Faulkner, published in 1898. East Fleet can be accessed from the Moonfleet Manor Hotel, a delightful place to take lunch, afternoon tea or dinner. There are several good circular walks around the lagoon. The more energetic could try the South West Coast Path from Ferry Bridge to Langton Herring, returning via Fleet, Charlestown and Wyke Regis.

hosts a large colony of Common Terns in the breeding season. As at Radipole, during the autumn migration time, large numbers of Swallows, Martins and Wagtails congregate here to feed before leaving for their winter quarters.

Sea Life Adventure Park "*has over 1,000 marine creatures and 5 rides and attractions.*" These include crocodiles, otters, Adventure Island, seals, the Ocean Tunnel, turtles, penguins, the Shipwreck, rock pools, rays, sharks, the Rainforest, Pirate Adventure Mini Golf, the Splash Zone and much more. It is a splendid family day out.

West of Weymouth there are several interesting places to visit. **Bennett's Water Gardens** are on the B3157 2mi (3km)

from the town centre. Covering 3ha of former clay pits, they have a large collection of Water Lilies, with a replica Monet Bridge. Grassy paths, woodland walks and convenient seats make a visit to the garden a delight, with its native and exotic trees, water plants, wild and garden flowers.

Wildlife here includes Grey Herons, Kingfishers, dragonflies and butterflies. The Tropical House has a range of cacti and exotic plants, while the museum tells the story of the gardens, Chickerell, Chesil Beach and The Fleet lagoon.

The Fleet lagoon is protected from the sea by Chesil Beach. In winter it attracts many wildfowl and waders to its mud banks and shallow waters. The

East of Weymouth the A353 offers fine views over Weymouth Bay, Bowleaze Point and the Purbeck coast. Northeast of Osmington (OE *Ōsmund-ington*, Osmund's Farm) the eponymous White Horse represents King George III leaving Weymouth. It was made in 1815 by removing the turf from the underlying chalk.

Osmington Mills is home to the Smugglers Inn, which originally dates from the 13th

East Fleet below Moonfleet Manor Hotel

Furzy Cliff and Bowleaze Cove

century. It belonged to the notorious smuggler, Emmanuel Charles in the early 19th century. No fewer than 27 of this family were convicted of smuggling, many of whom became wealthy enough to be on the electoral roll and have a vote.

Ringstead (OE h*ring-stede*, Ring Place) is a tiny village at the end of a toll road off the A353. The charge is worth paying for the views over Ringstead Bay to dramatic cliffs beyond. The beach here is variable with shingle, pebbles and sand. At low tide extensive offshore rocks are revealed.

Burning, or Holworth Cliff suffered a major landslip in 1825. The next year, it started to smoke and in May 1827 the cliff suddenly erupted in flame. It was described as, *"like a miniature Vesuvius, converting Weymouth Bay by day and night into a closer resemblance to the Bay of Naples than ever before contemplated by travellers"*. The fire burnt itself out in 1829.

Such fires are caused by iron pyrites being suddenly exposed to the air and igniting oil-rich shale. Similar events occurred in 1973 when parts of the cliff became red hot. The fire burned for several weeks at temperatures of over 500C. In 2000 there was a rock fall onto the beach which also ignited and burned for a similar time.

The White Nothe (SY772806, 167m) is a dramatic chalk headland, the start of the Pur-

Winter sunset over Weymouth Bay from the White Nothe

beck cliffs that run all the way to the Old Harry Rocks. In summer this area of calcareous chalk grassland and herbrich turf has a wide range of chalkland wild flowers. Butterflies include the Lulworth Skipper and Chalk-hill Blue.

Walks The whole area from Furzy Cliff to the White Nothe is excellent for walking. Whether starting from Osmington Mills, the White Nothe National Trust carpark or Furzy Cliff in the west, the Smuggler's Inn makes a fine stopping point for refreshments or to eat.

The "Smuggler's Path" down the White Nothe is very steep and only for those with a head for heights. Apart from this

the South West Coast Path and the many small lanes are easygoing and offer many possible circular routes.

The Osmington White Horse

Ringstead Bay, Burning Cliff and the White Nothe

THE NOTHE FORT, WEYMOUTH

The semi-circular interior of the Nothe Fort from the southwest

The Nothe Fort (OE *hnop*, nose, hill) dominates the large knoll on the south entrance to Weymouth harbour. A gun battery was installed here by Henry VIII. His successor made improvements when it became known as Queen Elizabeth's Fort.

The current impressive fort was built between 1860 and 1872 as part of the coast defences of Portland Harbour, then a rapidly expanding Royal Navy base. The magazine was on the bottom floor with about 70 rooms leading off a circular tunnel. The second level housed 12 large muzzle-loading cannons and their gun crews, while the top was open ramparts for close fighting.

Originally a mix of 64 pounders, 9-inch and 10.5-inch RML cannons were installed. Though muzzle-loaded, these had spiral-grooved barrels and a reasonably accurate range of about 3.5mi (5.5km). Around 1890, 12.5-inch cannons were installed which could fire 800lb shells the same distance.

Before WWI these cannons were replaced with three 6-inch quick-firing muzzle-loading guns. These fired 100lb armour-piercing shells over 10mi and became standard at many British coast defence batteries. The Royal Navy Home Fleet was despatched to Scapa Flow in Orkney early in the war due to its vulnerability and so the fort saw no action.

During the lead up to WWII the Nothe was modified to act as a major depot for anti-air-craft ammunition. A Vickers pom-pom and later a Bofors 40mm cannon was mounted as AA defence. Nothe Gardens had four 3.7-inch Vickers AA guns and searchlights for the air defence of Weymouth, which was bombed over 50 times by the Luftwaffe.

By 1961 the Royal Navy had no further need for coast defence batteries and the Nothe was sold to Weymouth & Melcombe Regis Borough Council. The lower level was transformed into a Cold War nuclear bunker, but the rest became derelict.

3.7-inch Vickers HAA gun

40mm Twin Bofors LAA gun

The Nothe Fort from Weymouth Pier

Since the late 1980s the fort has been renovated and turned into the hugely impressive visitor attraction that it is today. Many original cannons, guns, WWII vehicles and other military artefacts are on display. The ramparts feature a variety of 20th century AA and coast defence guns, while the second level has displays of very large 19th century cannon, complete with shells and realistic dioramas with their gun crews.

Vickers 6-inch MkVII coast defence gun

The fort is said to be haunted by a mystery phantom gunner who whistles in the many underground passages and rooms. It has the reputation of being one of the most spooky places in Britain. Special ghost hunting workshops are among the many events held here.

RML cannon with gun crew diorama

RML Cannon on mounting with shells

Viewpoints The Nothe Fort and Gardens offer several very fine views over Weymouth, Portland Harbour and Portland. The South Pier, which extends over 200m from the Nothe, also provides fine vistas over the harbour, seafront and bay as well as being a good sea-angling spot.

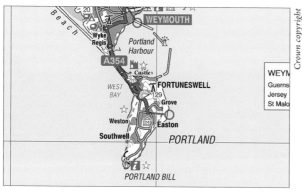

The view

THE ISLE OF PORTLAND (OE *port land*, land sheltering the port, popn 2011, 12,844) is an island joined to the mainland by the natural 2mi (3km) shingle barrier of Chesil Beach. It is composed mostly of oolitic Limestone from the Jurassic period. The Isle is about 4mi (6km) long and part of the South West Coast Path circumnavigates nearly all of it.

Because of the bulk of Portland, Weymouth Bay is sheltered from all directions except the east. Sailing ships heading down the English Channel could wait here for favourable winds to avoid the dangers of the Shambles Bank and tide race off Portland Bill.

Portland Stone consists of vast numbers of minute calcite balls, cemented together with precipitated calcite to form an ideal building stone. It is a freestone, easy to work, yet very resistant to weathering. It was first exploited commercially by the Romans, although it was used as a building material in Mesolithic times, at least 8,000 years ago, at Culverwell.

Quarrying and mining continues today. Portland Stone has been used all over Britain, especially in London, since at least the 14th century. Its use in the Banqueting House and the new St Paul's Cathedral made the stone very fashionable from the 17th century onwards. It re-

mains very popular today as a decorative finish.

Portland Castle was built in 1539 at a cost of £5,000. It is one of the "Device Forts" built under Henry VIII to provide coast defence in case of invasion by the French or Spanish. Today it is maintained by English Heritage. This fort is the oldest, but far from the grandest military structure here.

The Royal Navy finally departed from Portland in 1999, after 151 years, leaving behind a vast military infrastructure. A massive redevelopment programme was started and the Weymouth & Portland Sailing

Portland Castle, built in 1539 as a "Device Fort"

Sea Samphire

Heights over Chesil Beach, The Fleet, Fortuneswell, Portland Harbour and Weymouth Bay is one of the iconic vistas of Dorset

Academy was opened in 2005. A large new marina as well as extensive shoreside facilities were also built. The sailing events for the 2012 Games were held at the academy, giving a major boost to the area.

Nature The Isle of Portland is also famous for its natural heritage. With its combination of an exposed coastal position, limestone rocks, old quarries and rugged coastline, combined with a mild and sunny climate, Portland is a haven for wildlife. Wild flowers are especially abundant here and attract many butterflies. Portland Bill is famous for migrating birds as well as occasional passing cetacean.

Fortuneswell from Portland Heights

Fortuneswell in the early 20th century

Fossils in Portland Stone

PORTLAND	
Bird Observatory	88
Broadcroft Quarry	90
Church Ope Cove	87
Culverwell	88
Easton	86
Fortuneswell	83
Pennsylvania Castle	87
Portland Bill	88
Portland Castle	82
Portland Harbour	84
Portland Museum	86
Portland Sheep	89
Rufus Castle	87
St Andrew's Church	87
St George's Church	86
Southwell	87
Tout Quarry	90
Verne Citadel	84
Weston	87

Portland Harbour in the late 19th century

PORTLAND HARBOUR is today a busy commercial port and marine leisure facility. An increasing variety of shipping uses the docks. These include cruise ships which were formerly rare visitors to Dorset.

The building of breakwaters was first mooted in 1794, but it was over a century before the harbour was complete. As is the case with the majority of huge military defensive works, it was obsolete well before it was finished. Developments in ships, guns, submarines, torpedoes and, above all, aircraft made the harbour untenable for most of the Royal Navy during WWI and WWII.

The Admiralty approved the concept in 1825, but it was 1848 before work began on the harbour. Thousands of convicts quarried the vast quantities of stone needed to build the 3mi (5km) of breakwaters. They enclose c.520ha, making Portland Harbour possibly the biggest man-made harbour in the world.

Three huge forts were constructed between 1860 and 1892. These include The Nothe in Weymouth, now a museum, the Breakwater Fort, now abandoned, and The Verne which became an HM Prison. Further guns were mounted at Blacknor and East Weares.

The Verne Citadel (OE *fergen*, hill with woods) was designed as an "impregnable" siege fortress to defend Portland Naval Base. As such it had bomb-proof casemates to accommodate up to 1,000 personnel, and was surrounded by a rock-cut ditch on two sides and cliffs on the north and east. By 1877 it was armed with rifled muzzle-loading (RML) guns of up to 12.5in calibre, but by 1906 it was disarmed and obsolete.

Parade at The Verne Citadel

The East Weare Battery

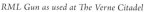

RML Gun as used at The Verne Citadel

East Weare and Verne High Angle Batteries, as well as Blacknor Fort, were built between 1863 and 1892 as outer defences for the Verne Citadel. They were armed with RMLs. Later, several breach-loading 9.2-inch and 6-inch guns were installed, some of which remained in place until 1956.

Verne High Angle Battery is open to the public (SY695732) and is accessed from a small carpark near the entrance to The Verne. The many tunnels can be explored with the aid of a torch and are occasionally the venue of Halloween events.

Portland Breakwater Fort, at the north end of the Outer Breakwater, was built during 1868-1875, but only armed in 1892. It is a circular iron structure on a granite base, designed to house 35 guns. In 1892 it had seven 12.5-inch RMLs, replaced in WWI by two 6-inch Vickers MkVII breach-loaders. Built at a cost of £76,000, it became known as *"Palmerston's Folly"*.

HM Portland Prison The Verne was an HM prison from 1949 to 2013. It is now an "Immigration Removal Centre", where detainees awaiting deportation are incarcerated. Prisons on Portland however go back to 1847, when temporary accommodation for convicts labouring on the harbour and forts was built at Grove Point. The former main entrance to the Verne Citadel is still impressive.

HM Prison on Portland

Prisoners on parade for gardening duties

Prisoners at work

Entrance to the Verne Citadel

St George's Church from the south

St George's Church, near Easton, is almost in the centre of Portland. This large, somewhat austere, church is the work of local mason, Thomas Gilbert. The design was inspired by St Paul's Cathedral, perhaps because his grandfather's firm quarried the stone for Wren's masterpiece.

Regarded by many as one of the most accomplished of Dorset's 18th century churches, it was built between 1754 and 1766. Abandoned in 1914, it was declared redundant in 1970 and is now in the care of the Churches Conservation Trust. It is also a Grade 1 listed building. The nearby George Inn was built for the parish clerk in 1767.

The spacious, mostly early 19th century, fixtures are in excel-

lent condition. These include twin pulpits; one for reading the scripture, the other for sermons. The box pews, three galleries, mouldering organ, and light interior all add to this impressive building.

The Easton Massacre The large surrounding graveyard is fascinating. The headstones commemorate people involved in shipwrecks, murders, piracy and smuggling. Perhaps the most interesting are those of Mary Way and William Lano, who were shot along with Alexander Andrews and Richard Flann by a press gang in 1803. The men were all killed by head shots, but the woman was shot in the back and died later of her injuries.

Three officers were tried for murder in Dorchester, Captain Wolfe and Lieutenant Hastings of HMS *L'Aigle*, and Lieutenant Jefferies of the Royal Marines, who had ordered his men to fire. The charge was that, *"while trying to impress men they caused their deaths"*. Despite eye witness testimony, the three accused were fully acquitted and released. The jury found that they had merely acted in self defence.

Portland Museum, in Wakeham, south of Easton, is housed in two 17th century cottages, one dated 1640. Founded in 1930 by Dr Marie Stopes, this little gem of a museum tells the story of Portland with displays on people, the sea, Portland Stone and fossils.

St George's Church interior from the gallery

The George Inn dates from 1767

Church Ope Cove and Rufus castle

Pennsylvania Castle

Church Ope Cove (OE *hop*, small bay) is accessed by a path near the Museum. It is named after the ruined St Andrew's Church, abandoned in 1753. Rufus, or Bow and Arrow, Castle stands on an outcrop above the bay. It was reputedly built for William II in the late 11th century but the ruins are 15th century. The grounds are occasionally open to the public.

Pennsylvania Castle was built for John Penn, grandson of William Penn, founder of Pennsylvania, between 1797 and 1800. This Gothic revival mansion is available for exclusive stays, special events and corporate use. During its time it has had many famous guests, not least Eisenhower and Churchill during the planning for D-Day, or so it is claimed.

Southwell is a large village with attractive 19th century cottages and an excellent pub, the Eight Kings. Nearby the extensive Combefield Quarries are still in operation, but they can be accessed in part. In 1734 the Southwell Landslip occurred on the east coast. It extended 1.5mi (2km) from Freshwater Bay to Durdle Pier.

West Coast The headland of Blacknor (OE *blæc ora*, black shore or bank), near Weston offers fine views along the whole west side of Portland. From the impressive 70m cliffs to the south, to the West Weare landslides and Chesil Beach this is a spectacular view. A raised beach, dating from 200,000 years ago, when sea level was about 15m higher, is clearly visible on this coast.

Church Ope Cove and Rufus castle

Portland Museum in Wakeham

Cliffs, landslip and raised beach from Blacknor

Portland Bill in 1822 by William Daniell

PORTLAND BILL is the most southerly point of Dorset. In former times it was a major danger to shipping due to the tide race which reaches 10 knotts during spring tides. Large eddies occur on both sides of Portland, causing tides to run south for 9 hours in each tide.

The Shambles is a sandbank 3mi (5km) southeast of Portland Bill. At low water spring tides there is less than 4m of water depth here. The race can extend right across this stretch of water, which has been the graveyard of many ships.

Culverwell There is a Mesolithic Settlement Site below Culverwell (SY685693) which is the earliest example so far found of built stone walls and floors. It dates to c.6000BC

and consists of a huge midden with four hearths in a sheltered gully. Large amounts of chert stone tools were found as well as debris from working the stone. Implements included microliths, knives, hammers, picks and scrapers. There were several such shelters in the area, with the Culverwell spring for fresh water.

Lighthouses In 1669 a patent was granted to erect a lighthouse here, but it was only in 1716 that the Higher and Lower Lighthouses were commissioned. In 1788 Portland was the first lighthouse to have Argand lamps installed, while in 1789 one of the towers was replaced. The obelisk was erected in 1844 as a mark for the Portland Shelf, which stretches 30m south of the Bill.

In 1869 the two lighthouses were rebuilt, and were in turn replaced by the present red and white tower in 1906. The station was automated in 1996. Today the lighthouse is open to the public with a visitor centre in the former keepers' accommodation.

Portland Bird Observatory is based in the Old Lower Light. This is one of the best places on the south coast of England for migrants. About 220 species of birds have been recorded here in recent times.

Pulpit Rock was created in 1870 by quarrying away the prized Portland Stone. Today it is a prime sea angling spot and viewpoint. The rocks here are full of fossils, especially molluscs. To the northwest the rugged low cliffs have blow holes, one at White Hole and another 500m further north.

Cave Hole, on the coast where the Culverwell Stream forms a waterfall in winter, is a partially collapsed cave, popular with climbers. It has an impressive blowhole. *Great care should be taken around all these features, especially in rough weather.*

Old Lower Lighthouse is now the Bird Observatory

Old Higher Lighthouse

The Portland Sheep is a primitive heathland British breed, which may go back to pre-Roman times. They are quite distinct from other ancient breeds such as Shetland Sheep, but relatively small, with tan-coloured faces. Both sexes have horn, those of the ewes form a crescent, while the rams may have double spirals.

Portland Bill Lighthouse from Pulpit Rock

Lambs are born with a red coat, which changes to creamy white in a few months. They produce a fine wool, well suited to hand-knitting. The Portland is unusual in that it can breed out of season, but normally produce only one lamb. The meat has an exceptional flavour and quality of texture.

Pulpit Rock

In 1086 there were 900 sheep on Portland. William the Conqueror held Portland directly and it was administered by the Manor Court. This ensured that the ancient system of land tenure lasted into the 20th century. Tenants hold narrow strips, which can still be seen today on the road to Portland Bill. The grazing of Common Land was controlled by strictly applied rules.

By 1840 there were over 4,000 sheep on Portland, but the coming of the Royal Navy and the HM Prison meant that much farmland was lost to buildings and quarries. In 1920 the last flock was sold at Dorchester. Due to the action of the Rare Breeds Survival Trust, the Portland Sheep is no longer threatened. There are now over 250 breeders in Britain.

Portland ram

Portland ewe and lamb

View northwest from Pulpit Rock

Tout Quarry is a Nature Reserve and Sculpture Park

DISUSED QUARRIES have evolved into nature reserves and sculptures parks. The base-rich soil of these abandoned industrial landscapes supports a special range of wild flowers. These include Pyramidal and Bee Orchids, Broomrapes, Autumn Gentian, Viper's Bugloss, Red Valerian and Yellow Vetchling.

Nature Reserves on Portland include Portland Tout (OE *tōt*, lookout hill), King Barrow, Broadcroft at Easton and Perryfields Quarries, near the Museum. The Verne High Angle Battery is also now a nature reserve. All of these sites require active management to prevent them being overwhelmed by encroaching scrub.

Butterflies Portland's old limestone quarries provide a wide variety of microclimates and habitats suitable for a range of butterflies. These include a number of species rare or absent elsewhere. The beautiful Silver-studded Blue is one of these. Its flying period is late June to early August.

The females lay their eggs on Birds-foot Trefoil. This species has a symbiotic relationship with Black Ants which look after the caterpillars and chrysalis before the emergence of imagos or adults.

In all, about 30 species of butterfly breed or occur here including Dingy Skipper, Grizzled Skipper, Marbled White, Small Copper, Common Blue, Chalkhill Blue, Grayling and Ringlet. Migratory species from the Continent also turn up here such as the Queen of Spain Fritillary.

Sculpture Park Tout Quarry is also home to a large number of sculptures. Stone carving courses are run here because Portland Stone is ideal for sculpture, as it is soft yet highly weather resistant. Many artists

Tout Quarry

Tout Quarry

Tout Quarry

Tout Quarry

have left permanent works in the park, while others have created temporary installations. Artefacts from quarry workings such as a bridge, trackways and part worked stone add further interest.

Flora Portland has a wide range of limestone-loving, salt-tolerant plants. The old quarry reserves, roadside verges, coastal path and herb-rich grassland near Portland Bill are good places to start. Portland Spurge, Rock Sea-lavender, Rock Samphire, Autumn Gentian, Red Valerian, and Viper's Bugloss are some of the many wild flowers prominent here.

The short grassland at the south end holds Pyramidal, Bee and a few Early-spider Orchids as well as Autumn Ladies' Tresses. Common, Ivy and Purple-flowered Broomrapes are also found on Portland.

Rabbits are the subject of an ancient superstition on Portland. It is considered taboo to refer to them by name, instead they are called "bunnies", "underground mutton" or "long-eared furry things". They were considered bad luck by

Silver-studded Blue female

Silver-studded Blue male

Brown Argus

Grayling

Steve Bound

quarry workers and fishermen alike. The fear of rabbits in quarry workings may well be due to their burrows causing landslides. Quarrying is a dangerous job and this may be the basis of the superstition.

Common Broomrape

Red Valerian

Viper's Bugloss

JURASSICA

Jurassica is a world-class new dinosaur theme park which is being planned for Yeolands Pit, in the disused Broadcroft limestone quarry near Easton on Portland. Covered by a 100m wide steel and glass roof, this underground geological park will have an aquarium with animatronic dinosaurs, as well as hundreds of fossil dinosaurs, marine reptiles, molluscs and plants found on the Jurassic Coast. It is hoped that this £90m project will open by 2020. "*Jurassica will be the world's most spectacular and up-to-date attraction celebrating the lost world of Prehistoric Earth. Jurassica will bring to a huge audience Britain's extraordinary scientific heritage and the unique role played by the County of Dorset in the birth of modern science and the understanding of evolution.*"

Burton Beach with Golden Cap on the left

1930sLondon & South Western Railway poster

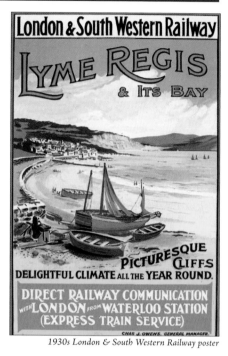

1930s London & South Western Railway poster

GETTING TO DORSET

With its central position on the southern coast of England, Dorset is easily accessible by air, road, rail and ferry from the UK, Ireland and Europe.

AIR TRAVEL

Dorset is served by four regional airports, which together offer services from nearly 200 places across the UK and Europe. The main airlines are easyJet, FlyBe, Ryanair and Thomson, but a host of other operators also offer flights.

Bristol Airport (BRS) BS48 3DY is 8mi south of Bristol on the A38
bristolairport.co.uk
Tel 0871 3344444

Bournemouth Airport (BOH) BH23 6SE is 4mi northeast of the town off the B3073
bournemouthairport.com
Tel 01202 364000

Exeter International Airport (EXT) EX5 2BD is 4mi east of the city off the A30
exeter-airport.co.uk
Tel 01392 367433

Southampton Airport (SOU) SO18 2NL is 4mi northeast of the city.
southamptonairport.com
Tel 0844 4817777

FERRIES

Dorset has now has only one operational ro-ro ferry port, at Poole, from which services run to France and the Channel Islands. Brittany Ferries operates from Poole to Cherbourg. Condor Ferries run services from Poole to Jersey and Guernsey, then onward to St Malo.
brittany-ferries.co.uk
condorferries.co.uk

RAIL TRAVEL

Dorset has excellent rail connections provided by three lines. These run from Waterloo to Weymouth, Weymouth to Exeter via Gillingham and Bristol to Weymouth. All of these lines go through Dorchester.

The First Great Western website is recommended for planning and booking as it does not

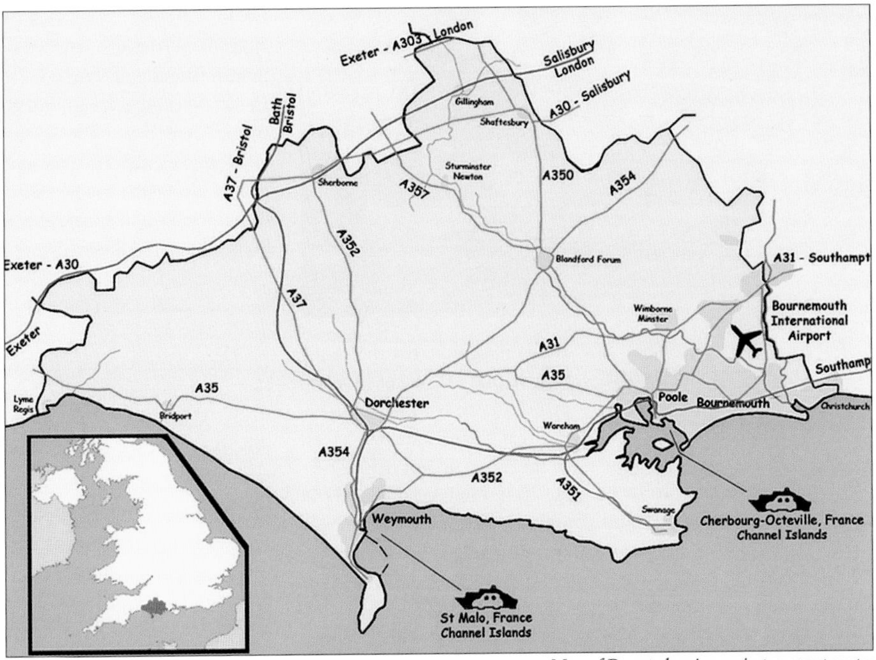
Exeter - A303
London
Salisbury
London
A30 - Salisbury
Bath
Bristol
A37 - Bristol
Gillingham
Shaftesbury
Sherborne
Sturminster Newton
A357
A350
A354
A352
Exeter - A30
Blandford Forum
A31 - Southampt
A37
Wimborne Minster
Bournemouth International Airport
Exeter
A31
A35
Southamp
Lyme Regis
A35
Bridport
Dorchester
Poole
Bournemouth
Christchurch
Wareham
A354
A352
A351
Swanage
Weymouth
Cherbourg-Octeville, France
Channel Islands
St Malo, France
Channel Islands

Wikipedia

Map of Dorset showing main transport routes

surcharge for credit cards, firstgreatwestern.co.uk Southwest Trains website, southwesttrains.co.uk and National Rail are also useful for planning nationalrail.co.uk

Freedom of the Severn-Solent is an excellent idea for those planning several journeys over a number of days. Passes are valid off peak during the weekend, all day at weekends and on Bank Holidays, railrover.org/pages/freedom-of-severn-and-solent-rover

ROAD TRAVEL

Although there are no motorways in Dorset, the county has excellent access to the national motorway system from London and the southeast, the north and the southwest.

easyJet
easyJet.com

easyJet flies to many destinations

FlyBe offers a wide range of UK and European destinations

flybe.

Getting Around in Dorset

The X53 bus in Bridport

Travel Within Dorset

DRIVING

Within Dorset there are sections of dual carriageway and many towns are bypassed. However during busy periods progress may be slow due to most of the roads being narrow and twisting as well as passing through small villages.

Accordingly, driving times between different parts of the county may be relatively long. With such a lot of beautiful scenery and so many places to visit, this should be regarded as a bonus to the visitor.

It is the quietness of the thousands of miles of narrow, single track lanes which wind between hedges across the countryside that are one of Dorset's principal attractions. However, great care needs to be taken as the locals do not drive slowly. Very large tractors, lorries and other traffic are frequently encountered.

BUSES

Dorset offers two special treats. The Route 50 Purbeck Breezer starts at Bournemouth train station then follows the coastline to Sandbanks. It then takes the chain ferry to Studland before ending up at Swanage. Open top buses are used on the year-round route.

The X53 Jurassic Coast Bus Service operates every two hours in the summer from Exeter via Sidford, Beer, Seaton, Lyme Regis, Charmouth, Bridport, Abbotsbury, Weymouth, Wool and Wareham to Poole. Tickets offer unlimited travel for a day. The service is ideal for walkers planning routes along the South West Coast Path. Full timetables at firstgroup.com/ukbus/dorset

CYCLING

Dorset offers a great deal to cyclists, however many of the main roads are not recommended. Most are narrow, with many blind summits and bends, and can be very congested at peak periods.

The good news is that the county has thousands of miles of delightful side roads and lanes to explore. Cycling is perhaps the best way to enjoy the Dorset countryside as the slow pace allows far more appreciation of the surroundings.

WALKING

The county is a paradise for all walkers, ranging from serious long distance types doing the South West Coast Path to those taking a short stroll. Walks are suggested through-

The many quiet lanes are great for cyclists

Dorset has many fingerposts

Walking on the Jurassic Coast

out the book and in the Itineraries Section. A variety of books about walking routes are included in the bibliography.

TRAVEL INFORMATION

The dorsetforyou.com website has a great deal of useful information about all forms of travel within the county. This includes car, bus, cycling, walking, rail, boat and air. The live travel alerts are especially useful: mapping.dorsetforyou.com/TravelDorset

Another excellent website for Dorset transport and travel information is dorset-transport.info. It offers live transport information on aircraft movements, trains and National Express coaches. Some buses also have tracking devices.

Dorset county sign

DISTANCES BY ROAD FROM DORCHESTER

WITHIN DORSET		mi	km
Dorchester	Blandford Forum	18	29
	Bournemouth	29	46
	Bridport	15	24
	Christchurch	34	56
	Exmouth	60	97
	Lyme Regis	26	42
	Poole	24	39
	Portland Bill	17	27
	Shaftesbury	31	49
	Sherborne	20	32
	Swanage	26	42
	Wareham	20	33
	Weymouth	9	14
NEARBY AIRPORTS		**mi**	**km**
Dorchester	Bournemouth Airport	29	46
	Bristol Airport	62	100
	Exeter Airport	55	89
	Gatwick	138	222
	Heathrow	111	178
	Luton Airport	144	232
	Southampton Airport	55	89
	Stansted	173	278
FERRY PORTS		**mi**	**km**
Dorchester	Dover	199	320
	Holyhead	339	546
	Hull	309	497
	Newcastle	379	609
	Pembroke	213	343
	Plymouth	99	159
UK TOWNS, CITIES AND PLACES		**mi**	**km**
Dorchester	Aberdeen	587	945
	Birmingham	169	273
	Bristol	62	100
	Edinburgh	457	735
	Exeter	55	89
	Inverness	612	985
	John o'Groats	728	1172
	Lands End	176	283
	London Centre	130	209
	London M25	113	182
	Salisbury	40	65
	Yeovil	21	34

West Dorset Places to Visit

What to See & Do in Dorset

Dorset offers the visitor a huge range of things to see and do within a relatively small area. Whatever your interest, whether it be archaeology, history, old churches and castles or nationally important formal gardens, it is here.

Museums The county features a large number of museums, from the world class Tank Museum to the tiniest specialist village heritage centre. All are interesting and staffed by enthusiastic people who love to tell the story of their museum.

The National Trust maintains a variety of properties here. These include Thomas Hardy's birthplace and his house in Dorchester. The grandiose mansion of Kingston Lacy is the creation of the Bankes family. Private mansions to visit include Athelhampton House and Sherborne Castle.

Nature enthusiasts will not be disappointed as the county is a year round destination for bird watchers. It is famous for its wild flowers, butterflies and dragonflies. With the 95mi (155km) long Jurassic Coast UNESCO World Heritage Site and nearly 60 varied nature reserves, there is plenty of scope.

Walkers will find Dorset very welcoming, with its huge network of paths, long distance and shorter. Routes can be planned by combining information in this guide with the relevant Ordnance Survey map. Alternatively there are many walking books available. Tour guides also lead groups in many places.

The Nine Stones, Winterborne Abbas

Cycling Cyclists will find the thousands of miles of winding hedge-lined lanes very enticing. There is no better way to observe the life of the countryside than on an ambling bike ride. The more energetic cyclist will find a large variety of suggested routes in leaflets at the VICs.

Activities For people who prefer more organised activities there is a wide range on offer, particularly in the vicinity of Poole, Bournemouth, Christchurch and Weymouth. These cover everything expected of prime seaside resorts with things to do for every age and inclination.

Coastline For many the prime attraction of Dorset is its coastline, with many superb beaches. Those at Poole, Bournemouth, Weymouth and Swanage have traditional seaside facilities and entertainments during the summer. People who prefer quiet coves or extensive beaches will not be disappointed, especially in the winter.

All-Year Attraction Dorset is a county which will reward the visitor at any time of year and in any weather. That so many visitors come back time and again is testament to the place, but also to the welcome afforded by the Dorset folk.

Accommodation This guide specifically does not cover information about accommodation, eating out or shopping as these are well covered by annual tourist guides and subject to frequent change. Dorset offers everything from five star hotels, self catering and bed & breakfast to campsites.

Eating Out ranges from top class restaurants to very good chip shops. Dorset offers an excellent range of local produce including prime beef, lamb, pork and seafood as well as fruit and vegetables in season. Few are disappointed.

Shopping The many small towns and villages have retained a wide selection of local shops. These include butchers, bakers, fish shops, drapers, bookshops, hardware stores, newsagents and antique outlets and other interesting businesses.

Maiden Castle

VISITOR INFORMATION CENTRES

visit-dorset.com

There are several Visitor Information Centres in Dorset, all in the main towns and villages. All can be found on visit-dorset.com This website is the Official Dorset Tourism Information Site and covers the huge range of things to see and do in Dorset.

Brochures may also be requested from this website covering Christchurch & Rural Dorset, West Dorset, Swanage & Purbeck as well as the main Dorset Guide.

Bridport Tourist Information Centre, Bucky Doo Square, South Square, Bridport DT6 3LF Tel 01308 424901

Dorchester Tourist Information Centre, Antelope Walk, Dorchester DT1 1BE Tel 01305 267992

Lyme Regis Tourist Information Centre, Church Street, Lyme Regis DT7 3BS 01297 442138

Sherborne Tourist Information Centre, Digby Road, Sherborne DT9 3NL Tel 01935 815341

Other information sources include visitor attractions, museums, local shops, accommodation providers and rural post offices. Books and guides are available from VICs, local bookshops and visitor attractions, as well as online.

ARCHAEOLOGY - NEOLITHIC

ARCHAEOLOGY - BRONZE AGE

ARCHAEOLOGY - IRON AGE

ARCHAEOLOGY - ROMANS

Charmouth Beach

Lyme Regis

Art & Craft

Tout Quarry Sculpture Park, Isle of Portland
Tel 01305 821638..90

Beaches, Coast & Cliffs

Boat Trips

Fleet Observer (Glass Bottom Boat), Wyke
Regis, Weymouth DT4 9NU
fleetobserver.co.uk Tel 01305 759692........76

Sherborne Abbey

Weymouth Whitewater, Nr town bridge,
Weymouth weymouth-whitewater.co.uk
Tel 0789 9892 317

Castles

Sherborne Castle, Sherborne DT9 5NR
sherbornecastle.com Tel 01935 813 182
Originally built by Walter Raleigh...............48

Sherborne Old Castle, Sherborne DT9 3SA
english-heritage.org.uk Tel 01935 812730
Slighted 11th century bishop's palace............48

Churches

Events & Festivals

Bridport Literary Festival bridlit.com Tel
01308 424901 Held annually in early November

Dorset Art Weeks dorsetartweeks.co.uk
Annually in late May and early June

Dorset County Show, Agriculture House,
Acland Road, Dorchester DT1 1EF
dorsetcountyshow.co.uk Tel 01305 264249
Annually in early September in the Showground
northeast of the town off the A35

Dorset Food Week
visit-dorset.com late October/early November

Lyme Lifeboat Week lymeregis.org Held in
July, culminates with the Red Arrows

Lyme Regis Fossil Festival
fossilfestival.com Tel 01297 445021
Held annually in the first week of May

Sandworld Sand Sculpture Festival,
Weymouth seafront sandworld.co.uk
Tel 07411 387 529 April to November

Sherborne Castle Country Fair
sherbornecountryfair.com Tel 01749 814041
Held annually in late May

Spirit of the Sea spiritofthesea.org.uk Tel
01749 814041In late May in Weymouth

Thomas Hardy Festival
hardysociety.org Tel 01305 251501
Held in late July/early August

Family Attractions & Activities

Abbotsbury Children's Farm, Church Street,
Abbotsbury DT3 4JJ abbotsburytourism.co.uk
Tel 01305 871817

Weymouth Sea Life Adventure Park, Pirate Adventure Mini Golf & **Model World,** Lodmoor
Country Park, Weymouth DT4 7SX sealifeweymouth.com Tel 01305 781 797 78

Gardens

Abbotsbury Sub-Tropical Gardens,
Abbotsbury, West Dorset DT3 4LA
abbotsburygardens.co.uk Tel 01305 871412
Old-established and very impressive 39

Athelhampton House Gardens, 5 miles east of
Dorchester off A35, DT2 7LG
athelhampton.co.uk Tel 01305 848363
One of the best gardens in England.............66

Bennett's Water Gardens, off A354 at
Weymouth onB3157 DT3 4AF
bennettswatergardens.com Tel 01305 785150
Former gravel pit............................78

Forde Abbey Gardens, nr. Thorncombe, West
Dorset TA20 4LU
fordeabbey.co.uk tel 01460 221290
Especially good in spring and autumn.........29

Kingston Maurward, off A35 east of Dorchester DT2 8PX
kmc.ac.uk/gardens Tel 01305 215003 66

Mapperton Gardens, nr Beaminster, West
Dorset DT8 3NR
mapperton.com Tel 01308 862645 29

The Nothe Fort, Weymouth

Minterne Gardens, Minterne Magna, on A352
north of Dorchester DT2 7AU
minterne.co.uk Tel 01300 341370..............45

Museums - Military

Portland Castle, Liberty Rd, Castletown,
Portland DT5 1AZ
english-heritage.org.uk/portland
Tel 01305 820 539   Well-preserved Henry
VIII "Device Fort"..........................82

The Keep Military Museum, Bridport Road,
Dorchester DT1 1RN
keepmilitarymuseum.org Tel 01305 264066
Devon & Dorset Regimental history...........57

The Nothe Fort, Barrack Road, Weymouth
DT4 8UF
nothefort.org.uk Tel 01305 766626
Impressive 19th century fort and museum 80

Museums - Main

Dorset County Museum, High West Street,
Dorchester DT1 1XA
dorsetcountymuseum.org Tel 01305 262735
Excellent and essential visit..........................56

Fossil fish in Charmouth Heritage Centre

Abbotsbury Swannery

MUSEUMS - SMALL & SPECIALIST

Beaminster Museum, Whitcombe Road, Beaminster DT8 3NB
beaminstermuseum.org Tel 01308 863623140

Bridport Museum, 25 South Street, Bridport DT6 3RJ bridportmuseum.co.uk
Tel 01308 458703... 32

Dinosaurland Fossil Museum, Coombe Street, Lyme Regis Tel 01297 443541
Tel 01747 823234

Lyme Regis Museum, Bridge Street, Lyme Regis DT7 3QA lymeregismuseum.co.uk
Tel 01297 443370... 21

Marine Aquarium and Cobb History, The Cobb, Lyme Regis 01297 444230

Mill House Cider Museum, Owermoigne DT2 8HZ Off A352 north of Owermoigne
millhousecider.com Tel 01305 852220
Fascinating old cider-making equipment 67

Portland Museum, 17 Wakeham, Portland DT5 1HS portlandmuseum.co.uk
Tel 01305 821804 small and interesting 86

Weymouth Sealife Adventure Tower

Sherborne Museum, 1 Church Lane, Sherborne DT9 3BP sherbornemuseum.co.uk
Tel 01935 812252...49

Teddy Bear Museum, Salisbury Street, Dorchester DT1 1JU teddybearmuseum.co.uk
Tel 01305 266040...59

Terracota Warriors Museum, Salisbury Street, Dorchester DT1 1JU terracotawarriors.co.uk
Tel 01305 268885...59

The Dinosaur Museum, Icen Way, Dorchester DT1 1EW thedinosaurmuseum.com
Tel 01305 269860...59

The Tutankhamun Exhibition, High West Street, Dorchester DT1 1UW
tutankhamun-exhibition.co.uk
Tel 01305 269571...59

Tolpuddle Martyrs Museum, Tolpuddle, Dorchester DT2 7EH
tolpuddlemartyrs.org.uk Tel 01305 848 237
The start of trade unions..............................69

Tudor House, 3 Trinity Street, Weymouth DT4 8TW dorsetmuseums.co.uk
Tel 01305 779711...75

NATURE

Abbotsbury Swannery, Abbotsbury DT3 4JG abbotsbury-tourism.co.uk Tel 01305 871858
Best in April and May to see the Mute Swans nesting - an essential visit...........................38

Dorset Wildlife Trust, Brooklands Farm, Forston, Dorchester DT2 7AA
dorsetwildlifetrust.org.uk Tel 01305 264620

Portland Bird Observatory and Field Centre, Old Lower Lighthouse, Portland Bill DT5 2JT
portlandbirdobs.org.uk Tel 01305 820553
Dorset's only Bird Observatory...................88

Radipole Lake RSPB Reserve, Weymouth DT4 7TZ rspb.org.uk Tel 01305 778313
Wetland reserve all year birding interest 77

NATURE - JURASSIC COAST

Charmouth Coastal Heritage Centre, Lower Sea Lane, Charmouth DT6 6LL
charmouth.org Tel 01297 560772
Excellent Jurassic Coast Centre 24

Chesil Beach Visitor Centre, Portland Beach Road, Portland DT4 9XE
dorsetwildlifetrust.org.uk/chesil-beach-centre
Tel 01305 206191...76

The Jurassic Coast, Dorset and East Devon World Heritage Site jurassiccoast.org Runs for 95mi (155km) from Orcombe Point near Exmouth to Old Harry Rocks in Purbeck

Jurassica *"will be the world's most spectacular attraction celebrating the lost world of Prehistoric Earth. There will be an aquarium, featuring animatronic Jurassic marine reptiles, the sea monsters of prehistoric Earth. There will be three galleries featuring fossil collections from the Natural History Museum and world-class specimens currently in the hands of private collectors."*
jurassica.org

Seaton Jurassic, Underfleet, Seaton, Devon EX12 2LX seatonjurassic.org is due to open in 2015 and will be *"the Jurassic Coast's newest and most exciting visitor experience, telling the story of its geology and ecology."*

VISITOR ATTRACTIONS

Cerne Abbas Giant, A352 from Dorchester
nationaltrust.org.uk tel 01297 489481
Famous landmark cut into a chalk hillside 44

Hardy's Monument and Viewpoint, Black Down, Portesham DT3 4ET
nationaltrust.org.uk Tel 01297 489481
Spectacular panoramic views.......................42

Mangerton Mill, Bridport DT6 3SG north of Bridport off the A 3066
visit-dorset.com Tel 01308 485224
Watermill, cafe and craft shops 33

Max Gate, Alington Avenue, Dorchester DT1 2AB off the A35 east of the town
nationaltrust.org.uk/max-gate/

Autumn Colours Marshwood Vale

Tel 01305 262538 Thomas Hardy's house......62

Old Crown Court and Cells, High West Street, Dorchester DT1 1UZ
visit-dorset.com Tel 01305 267992 Where the Tolpuddle Martyrs were tried 56

Palmers Brewery, West Bay Road, Bridport DT6 4JA palmersbrewery.com
Tel 01308 422 396 Tours & Visitor Centre....32

Portland Bill Lighthouse, Portland DT5 2JT
trinityhouse.co.uk Tel 01305 820495
Panoramic view from the tower 88

Thomas Hardy's Cottage, Higher Bockhampton, Dorchester DT2 8QJ
nationaltrust.org.uk/hardys-cottage/
Tel 01305 262366
Atmospheric cottage and garden.................62

Town Mill, Lyme Regis DT7 3PU
townmill.org.uk Tel 01297 443579............22

Weymouth Sea Life Tower, Festival Pier, Weymouth DT4 8DX
weymouth-tower.com
Panoramic views of Weymouth...................76

Hardy's Cottage, Higher Bockhampton

What to See and Do in Dorset
Some Suggested Itineraries

This guide describes a large number of places to visit throughout the area. The following itineraries make many suggestions to help visitors plan their time, depending on interests, weather, season and locality. All of the main attractions, walks, viewpoints and many places of interest are included as well as mini-indexes and distances.

4. Sherborne & Around 112

2. Beaminster & Marshwood Vale p108

3. Abbotsbury & Inland p110

1. Lyme Regis to Bridport - p106

5. Dorchester & Around p114

6. Weymouth p116

7. Portland p118

COUNTRYSIDE CODE

Please observe these guidelines:

1. Always use stiles and gates, and close gates behind you.
2. Always ask permission before entering farmland.
3. Keep to paths and avoid fields of grass and crops.
4. Do not disturb livestock.
5. Take your litter away with you and do not light fires.
6. Do not pollute water courses.
7. Never disturb nesting birds.
8. Do not pick wild flowers or dig up plants.
9. Drive and park with care and attention, do not obstruct or endanger others, park responsibly.
10. Take care near cliffs and beaches, particularly with children and pets. Some beaches are dangerous.
11. Walkers should take adequate clothes, wear suitable footwear and tell someone of their plans.
12. Above all, please respect the life of the countryside - leave only footprints, take only photographs and pleasant memories.
Notice: Most of the sites in this guide are open to the public and have marked access; many are on private land. No right of access is implied; if in doubt it is always polite to ask. Many roads and tracks are rights of way, but not all are.

SOME SUGGESTED ITINERARIES

WHAT TO DO AND SEE A selection of suggested itineraries is included in the following pages. Each is designed to take a day, with plenty of time for getting there, exploration and a picnic or meal along the way.

Private Transport The itineraries assume the use of a car to reach the places mentioned during the course of a day. Many could also be done by bicycle or by a combinaton of public transport and walking, though this would take longer.

Public Transport The dorsetforyou.com website has a great deal of information about all forms of travel within the county, including by car, bus, cycling, walking, rail, boat and air. The live travel alerts are especially useful: mapping.dorsetforyou.com/TravelDorset

Access to the Outdoors is available at all times at the sites mentioned. Most of the visitor attractions charge for entry. Some, very helpfully, include multiple visits for a year. Many have seasonal opening. Websites, addresses, postcodes and phone numbers are listed on pages 100-105.

Car Parking is charged for throughout Dorset, even at seemingly remote sites. Membership of the National Trust and the RSPB is strongly recommended. Permits are available, but there is no comprehensive scheme for the whole county, making them of little use to visitors. It is strongly recommended to have a good supply of £1 coins.

Walking Dorset is a walker's paradise, with thousands of miles of quiet country lanes, byways, tracks, holloways and footpaths. This guide does not suggest detailed walking routes as exploring is half of the delight of any visit. For those wishing such directions there is a good selection of walks books available. Most attractions stock leaflets giving current details of opening times, prices, walks, etc.

Country Lanes Dorset has thousands of miles of highly attractive country lanes. These are usually narrow, winding, hedge-lined and have few passing places. Locals tend to drive quite fast, while traffic may include huge tractors, cattle, sheep, cyclists and pedestrians. All road users should proceed with care and attention, no matter how rural and quiet the road might appear.

Although not specifically mentioned in the itineraries, the verges, hedges and field boundaries throughout Dorset are a haven for wildlife, including wildflowers, birds, butterflies and mammals.

Maps The use of OS Explorer 1:25,000 or OS Landranger 1:25,000 maps, or their digital equivalent, is assumed. The 1:25,000 scale maps are by far the best for exploration as they provide excellent detail.

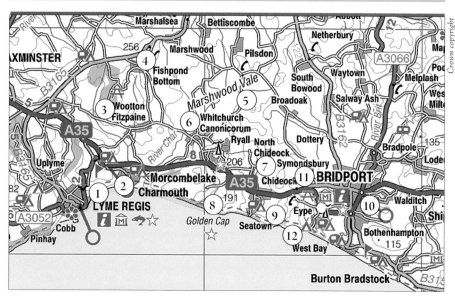

Crown copyright

LYME REGIS TO BRIDPORT

The western extremity of West Dorset includes some of the most spectacular coastal and inland scenery in the whole county. The Jurassic Coast includes cliffs, undercliffs, beautiful beaches and sweeping views. Inland, narrow hedge-lined lanes wander through lush undulating farmland.

Lyme Regis (popn. 2011, 3,671) is a quintessential little English seaside resort, nestling in the shelter of a steep-sided valley. With its ancient winding streets, small harbour sheltered by The Cobb, seafront, many interesting shops, cinema and theatre it offers much to the visitor.

Bridport (popn. 2011, 13,568) is larger, but has an equally long history. Built along the old Roman road to Exeter above the confluence of the Rivers Brit and Asker, it has long been

a centre for ropemaking. Today, along with its harbour at West Bay, it is a vibrant town with many independent shops and a strong cultural scene.

Charmouth (popn. 2011, 1,352) has a particularly fine beach which is especially good for fossil hunting. The Heritage Coast Centre here is a must for everyone interested in fossils and dinosaurs.

Other villages include Wootton Fitzpaine, Morecobelake, Whitchurch, Seaton, Chideock and Eype. All have their own sites of interest, natural or historical. This seemingly remote corner of Dorset is in fact, brimming with things to see and do.

The coast can be accessed from numerous places here, offering a wide range of possibilites for circular walks.

ORDNANCE SURVEY 1:50,000 & 1:25,000 MAPS

OS Landranger Map 193   Taunton & Lyme Regis
OS Explorer Map 116   Lyme Regis & Bridport

LYME REGIS TO BRIDPORT

1. Lyme Regis (page 20) is an all-year tourism destination. In summer the beach is great for family swimming and seaside activities, while in winter storms huge waves break over The Cobb. There are events and festivals throughout the year. Lyme is a delightful place to explore at a slow pace on foot.

The Spittles (page 22) are the eroding cliffs to the east of Lyme Regis. A new sea wall and promenade has been built to protect the eastern part of the town from subsidence. It forms part of a fine 1.5mi (2km) beach walk to Charmouth. *This should only be attempted on a falling tide.*

Undercliff (page 22) form a National Nature Reserve for 7mi (11km) from Lyme Regis to Axmouth. An undulating path passes through a magical world of landslips, with woodland, streams, small valleys and areas of grassland. Please note that this route is sometimes closed due to new landslips.

2. Charmouth Beach (page 24), along with Monmouth and The Spittles Beaches, is perhaps the best place to look for fossils on the Jurassic Coast. The best time is at low tide after a storm has washed out new landslips. Ammonites and belemnites are easy to find but Ichthyosaur teeth and bones may also get revealed. The gently shelving sand and shingle beach is excellent for swimming. The shore can be walked all the way to Seatown *at low tide* 4mi (6km). St Gabriel's Steps give access to Golden Cap and Stonebarrow Hill from the beach 2mi (3km) east of Charmouth.

The Heritage Coast Centre (page 24) above the Char estuary has hands-on collections of fossils and runs fossil-collecting tours on the beach.

Stonebarrow Hill (page 24) is about 1.5mi from the centre of Charmouth up Stonebarrow Lane. From here paths lead to Golden Cap 1.5mi (2km).

3. Wootton Fitzpaine (page 25) is famous for its displays of Wild Daffodils, Cowslips, Wood Anemones, Bluebells, Green-winged and other Orchids in springtime. The meadows off Westover Hill, Thistle Hill woodlands and the path to Charmouth are the best places to look.

4. Coney's Castle (page 28) is on Long Lane 1mi (1.5km) north of Wootton Fitzpaine. This small Iron Age hillfort is famous for its drifts of Bluebells in spring and autumn colours later in the year.

Lambert's Castle (page 28) is about 0.8mi (1km) further north. This extensive hillfort is covered with mature trees, many mysteriously shaped, and offers expansive views over Marshwood Vale

5. Marshwood Vale (page 28) is mostly sparsely populated farmland meadows, criss-crossed by many narrow, hedge-lined lanes which are interesting to explore on foot or by bicycle.

6. Whitchurch (page 26) is a small village on the south side of Marshwood Vale with a fascinating old church which is well worth visiting for its unique Shrine and interesting headstones.

7. Chideock (page 26) has many beautiful thatched houses, but is marred by the busy A35. For those on a long circular walk, it offers two excellent pubs.

8. Golden Cap (page 25, 26) can be reached by small lanes and footpaths from Langdon Hill, Chideock or Seatown, 1mi (1.5km). At 191m it is the highest point on the south coast and offers spectacular panoramic views of Lyme Bay.

9. Seatown (page 27) is about 900m south of Chideock down a narrow lane. With its shingle beach, spectacular cliffs and fine old pub it is a good stopping place. There is a fine clifftop walk to West Bay from here 3mi (5km), passing Thorncombe Beacon (page 25) and Eype's Mouth (page 35).

10. Bridport (page), with its wide main streets and many old buildings, is well worth exploring on foot. There are many independent shops, pubs and restaurants as well as a vibrant cultural scene.

11. Colmer's Hill (page 27) is a prominent conical landmark topped with a few pines. It can be reached from Symondsbury or North Chideock and offers an excellent panoramic view.

Symondsbury (page 27), just northwest of Bridport, has interesting old buildings, now renovated. Mysterious old holloways go into the countryside from here into a world seemingly far away.

12. West Bay (page 34), Bridport's harbour, is 2mi (3km) from the town centre. Spectacular clifftop walks go west to Seatown and Charmouth, or east to Burton Bradstock. The beach is shingle and hard to walk far on. Stalls sell delicious fish and chips, while there are excellent pubs and restaurants.

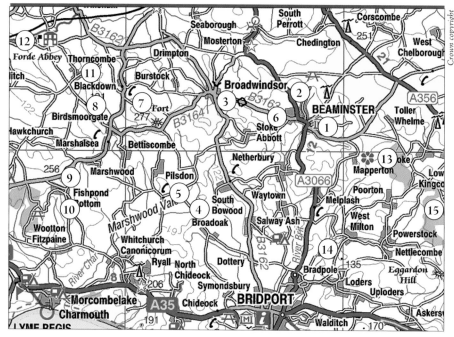

Crown copyright

Marshwood Vale (OE *mersc wudu*, marshy wood) is a large oval valley, surrounded by higher ground, except to

the southeast. It is formed of Lower Lias clay which is relatively impermeable, hence the marshy ground. The source of the River Char is in the north of the Vale.

The area has escaped much of the march of modern intensive farming and retains its ancient pattern of irregular small fields. It is traversed by many narrow, sinuous, hedge-lined lanes and age-old footpaths. The low-lying valley was originally forested, and several small stands of ancient woodland remain in places. The area is especially mysterious on misty, frosty winter mornings.

Hillforts Marshwood Vale is ringed by Iron Age hillforts, many of which were in use since Neolithic times or earlier. Lewesdon Hill (272m) is the

highest in Dorset, closely followed by Pilsdon Pen (277m) and Lambert's Castle (256m). All three have large, multivallate hillforts and afford spectacular panoramic views across the valley.

Beaminster lies to the northeast of the Vale in its own small bowl-shaped valley. Far from main roads and the railway this attractive little settlement has preserved its attractive local limestone centre and escaped the near ubiquitous chain store conformity of so many.

The town was prosperous during the 18th and 19th centuries, producing linen and wool. It is said that there were once 17 inns here. The oldest still standing is the Bridge House Hotel, which originally dates from the 13th century.

ORDNANCE SURVEY 1:50,000 & 1:25,000 MAPS

OS Landranger Map 193	Taunton & Lyme Regis
OS Explorer Map 116	Lyme Regis & Bridport

BEAMINSTER & MARSHWOOD VALE

1. Beaminster (page 28, popn. 2011, 3,136) is 5mi (8km) north of Bridport on the A3066) at the head of the Brit Valley. An attractive little town rebuilt in yellow limestone; it was burnt by the Royalists in 1644, as well as by accident in 1684 and 1781, then finally rebuilt in local stone. With over 200 listed buildings, a wide selection of local shops and accommodation, it makes a good base.

2. Horn Hill Tunnel (page 28), on the A3066 1.5mi (2km) north of Beaminster. was opened in 1832 to bypass the very steep Horn Hill. The 105m-long tunnel is still in use.

3. Broadwindsor (page 29) is 2mi (3km) west of Beaminster. The Craft and Design Centre is based in renovated old farm buildings and is home to artists' and crafts studios, shops selling food, drink, toys and all manner of gifts as well as a restaurant.

4. Marshwood Vale (page 28) is largely unpopulated, due to being composed of impermable Lower Lias clay. It is criss-crossed by many narrow, hedge-lined lanes which are interesting to explore on foot or by bicycle. Some small areas of ancient woodland harbour rare plants.

5. Shave Cross Inn (OE *sceaga*, copse or grove, SY415980) is an excellent and deservedly popular pub, centrally placed for food and refreshments.

6. Waddon Hill (page 29, 207m, ST448015) has a Roman fort which was occupied during 50-60AD. Artefacts may be seen in Bridport Museum.

Lewesdon Hill (page 29, 279m) is the highest point in Dorset. Like Pilsdon Pen it is formed from erosion resistant Upper Greensand and has a hillfort, now hidden by woodland.

7. Pilsdon Pen (page 28, 277m, ST413011) is the largest of several hillforts which surround Marshwood Vale. There are spectacular panoramic vistas in all directions from here.

8. Birdsmoorsgate (page 109) is on a high ridge at the crossroads of the B3165 and B3164. There are fine views over Pilsdon Pen and Marshwood Vale.

9. Lambert's Castle (page 28) is about 2mi (3km) southwest of The Birdsmoorgate crossroads. This extensive hillfort is covered with mature trees, many mysteriously shaped, and offers expansive views over Marshwood Vale.

10. Coney's Castle (page 29) is on Long Lane 1mi (1.5km) north of Wootton Fitzpaine. This small Iron Age hillfort is famous for its drifts of Bluebells in spring and autumn colours later in the year.

11. Thorncombe (page 29, ST375033) is a small village near Forde Abbey. The present church was opened in 1867, but includes artefacts from the previous medieval building, including a large memorial brass to Sir Thomas and Lady Brooke, who died in 1417 and 1437. He was much in favour with Henry IV and a Member of the Commons.

12. Forde Abbey (page 29, ST362052) stands in a prominent position on the south side of the River Axe. It was founded in the 1130s as a Cistercian Abbey, taking its name from a nearby ford across the river and eventually its estate extended to over 12,000ha. Parts of the abbey church and building were demolished after 1539, but much remains, creating an interesting grand house. The gardens cover 12ha and include several water features. They are open all year along with the tearoom and plant nursery. In spring huge drifts of Daffodils, followed by Bluebells, are spectacular. The gardens are also famous for their autumn colours.

13. Mapperton House & Gardens (page 29, SY503997) is about 2mi (3km) east of Beaminster off the B3163. The enchanting 17th century sandstone manor house and outbuildings may be visited in the summer. The gardens are in a sheltered valley and are open from March to October. The house is said to be one of the best of its kind in England.

14. Mangerton Mill (page 33, SY490058) is a partially restored watermill and museum off the A3066 about 2mi (3km) north of Bridport. There is an excellent tearoom as well as art and craft studios and a small lake. Open from April to October.

15. Powerstock Common (page 42, SY547974) between Bridport and Maiden Newton is one of the best nature reserves in Dorset. It includes a stretch of abandoned railway line as well as woodland, wetland and grassland. It is at its best in early summer for various species of orchids, butterflies, dragonflies and breeding birds. In spring the woodland floors are a mass of Bluebells. Parking is next to an old railway bridge on Barrowland Lane.

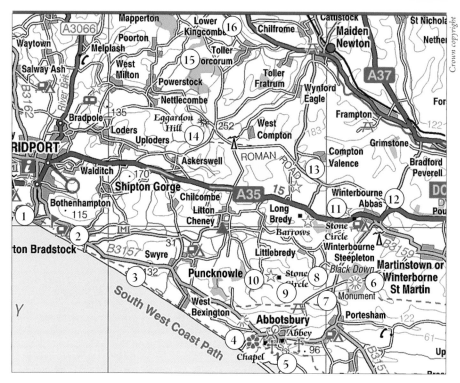

Crown copyright

ABBOTSBURY lies at the centre of a part of Dorset where the visitor is spoilt for choice. The only answer is to keep coming back for more. There are dramatic views from everywhere along the B3167 coast road, but one of the best vistas in Dorset is undoubtedly from the steep hill west of the village.

Stop in one of the several laybies and take time to savour the The Fleet and Chesil Beach, with Portland behind, St Catherine's Chapel in the foreground and Abbotsbury nestling in its valley. Probably the best time to visit is early morning or evening in the winter.

Chesil Beach is an immemse shingle barrier stretching from West Bay to Portland. The size of the pebbles is graded from west to east, starting off with pea-sized stones and gradually increasing in diameter the further east one goes. There is limited access to The Fleet lagoon except where the South West Coast Path follows the northern shore from Langton Herring to Ferrybridge.

The Ridgeway passes along the Chalk spine which runs from Askerswell Down and on to Purbeck. Large numbers of prehistoric sites litter this area, which is dominated by Black Down with its prominent Hardy's Monument. There are countless quiet lanes, footpaths and tracks to explore, each revealing more fine views.

ORDNANCE SURVEY 1:50,000 & 1:25,000 MAPS

OS Landranger Map 194   Dorchester & Weymouth
OS Explorer Map OL15   Purbeck & South Dorset

ABBOTSBURY & INLAND

1. Chesil Beach (page 38), a shingle barrier beach, stretches 18mi (29km) from West Bay to Portland. It is up to 200m wide and 15m high and is very hard walking. The South West Coast Path follows the beach all the way from West Bay to Abbotsbury.

2. Burton Bradstock (page 38) marks the end of the dramatic sandstone cliffs that run from here to Golden Cap. The very popular Hive Beach Cafe overlooks Hive Beach.

3. Cogden Beach (page 38), in contrast, is wholly uncommercialised. It is reached via several meadows, which abound in wild flowers in spring and summer. The beach is also host to many plants and is backed by small lagoons, with water plants, amphibians and breeding birds. In spring and autumn this is an excellent place to seek migrant birds.

4. Abbotsbury (page 38) is a highly attractive little village which nestles in a small valley overlooking The Fleet and Chesil Beach. The village and environs have much to offer the visitor.

Abbotsbury Castle (page 38, 215m, 2ha) is a small hillfort on Wears Hill to the west of the village. It has a panoramic view of Lyme Bay.

Abbotsbury Sub-Tropical Gardens (page 39, 8ha) have many rare and exotic flowers, including world famous Camellia groves and Magnolias.

St Catherine's Chapel (page 39) is very prominent on the top of Chapel Hill, south of the village. It is barrel-vaulted and dates from the 14th century.

Abbotsbury Swannery (page 38) is said to be "*The world's only managed colony of nesting Mute Swans.*" The best time is May and June when the cygnets are hatching, but the site is open from March to October. Swans and wildfowl are present all year.

5. The Fleet (page 39) is a tidal lagoon which stretches from Abbotsbury to Ferrybridge.

6. Hardy's Monument (page 41, SY614877, 242m) is sited very prominently on the summit of Black Down. It commemorates Thomas Masterman Hardy, Nelson's captain at Trafalgar. This site offers splendid views in all directions.

Archaeological sites are present in abundance in the area north of Portesham. Bronze Age tumuli are abundant along this chalk ridge from Long Bredy to Bincombe Hill north of Weymouth. There are extensive footpaths and lanes all over this area.

7. Hellstone (page 40) is about 1,000m southeast of Hardy's Monument. This large neolithic chambered cairn was set up as it is seen now in 1866.

8. The Valley of the Stones (page 40, signposted west of Hardy's Monument) is a chalk combe famous for its large sandstone Sarsen stones which litter the valley floor.

9. The Grey Mare & Her Colts (page 40, SY584870) is reached by a 500m footpath off the road from Abbotsbury to Black Down. This impressive Neolithic chambered cairn is the best in Dorset.

10. Kingston Russell Stone Circle (page 40) is about 800m northwest of the Grey Mare along the same path. This small oval setting has 18 recumbent monoliths and is aligned to the midwiner sunset.

11. The Nine Stones Circle (page 40) stands on the busy A35 500m west of Winterborne Abbas. Access to this impressive stone circle is from the nearby Little Chef carpark.

12. Roman Road (page 42) A long stretch of Roman road can be traced from east of Dorchester to Eggardon Hill and part of the way to Bridport. The section from Lambert's Hill (SY633907) to the hillfort follows a quiet and very scenic side road.

13. Compton Valence (page 43, SY595932) is a hamlet in a small, sheltered valley just north of the Roman road. In early spring it has a profusion of Snowdrops, followed by Daffodils.

14. Eggardon Hill (page 42, SY541947, 252m, 8ha) is a small hillfort on a chalk ridge prominently situated off Spyway Road 5mi (8km) east of Bridport. There are panoramic views in all directions from the impressive ramparts. The hill is famous for its orchids and butterflies in summer.

15. Powerstock Common see page 109.

16. Kingcombe Meadows (page 43, SY553990, 185ha) is about 1mi (1.5km) north of Toller Porcorum. Kingcombe Visitors Centre is signposted off Kingcombe Road. The reserve is in the River Hooke valley with a clay bottom and Greensand on the lower slopes, while chalk caps the northern side. The grassland is grazed, or cut for hay, while hedges, lanes, streams and marshy areas complete the diversity. Over 430 species of wild flowers have been recorded here. There are marked trails to explore this very impressive wildlife reserve.

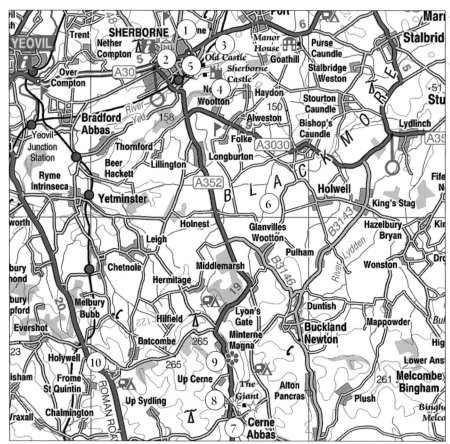

Crown copyright

Sherborne lies in a salient of West Dorset which extends to the River Yeo in the west to Poyntington Hill about 5mi (8km) to the east. Although there are no significant archaeological sites to visit in the vicinity, there is evidence of much activity in the area during the Iron Age and Roman times. The dairy at Sherborne Castle, somewhat bizarrely, has a resited Roman mosaic floor.

Its beautiful situation has inspired many famous people, including the Saxon kings who made it the capital of the Kingdom of Wessex. They established Sherborne Abbey, as well as the original school.

Later, the Normans built Sherborne Old Castle on a prime site. This was ruinous when Sir Walter Raleigh first saw it on his way from London to Plymouth. His heart became set on building a country lodge here for his wife, Elizabeth and himself.

Sherborne Museum has an excellent small collection of local artefacts dating from the Palaeolithic Age to recent times. One of the highlights of the museum is an electronic version of the 15th century Sherborne Missal. This was produced by the Benedictine Monastery in the international gothic style and is an exquisite example of this style of book illustration.

ORDNANCE SURVEY 1:50,000 & 1:25,000 MAPS

OS Landranger Map183, Dorchester & Weymouth; Map 194, Yeovil & Frome
OS Explorer Map 129, Yeovil & Sherborne; Map 117, Cerne Abbas & Bere Regis

SHERBORNE & AROUND

1. Sherborne (page 48, popn. 2011, 9,523) occupies a fine south-facing slope on a tributary of the River Yeo and has been claimed to be *"the most attractive town in the county."* It has a long history going back to Saxon times and is largely built of local ochre-coloured Ham Stone. The town centre has a wide range of independent shops, art and antique dealers, as well a a good selection of restaurants and pubs. There is a large network of quiet lanes, tracks and footpaths to explore roundabout.

2. Sherborne Abbey, or St Mary's Church, (page 50) was founded in AD705 and is one of the most outstanding churchs in Dorset. The building only survived due to the determination of the people of the town after the Dissolution of the Monasteries in 1539. Today it is an essential visit, especially to see the exquisite 15th century fan-vaulted roof of the nave. The building includes Saxon, Norman and Medieval features, all of which combine to make a very fine church.

St John's Almshouse (page 50) is across the green from the church and dates from the 15th century. The chapel is original with a fine stained glass window and a triptych which may have come from Cologne. **The Close** gives fine views of the abbey, while **the Conduit** on Cheap Street is now a market house, having been the *lavatorium* of the monastery.

3. Sherborne Old Castle (page 48) occupies a fine site to the east of the town overlooking Sherborne Lake. It was built by the Norman, Roger de Caen in the early 12th century as a fortified bishop's palace. Most of the ruins date from this time apart from work carried out by Walter Raleigh in the 1590s after being given the Sherborne Estate by Elizabeth I. The Castle was twice besieged by the Parliamentarians during the Civil War. The second was led by Cromwell himself, who called it *"A malicious mischievous Castle"*, before having it slighted. The site is maintained by English Heritage.

4. Sherborne (New) Castle (page 48) is off New Road, southeast of the town. It was originally built by Sir Walter Raleigh in the 1590s as Sherborne Lodge. The central block and polygonal corner towers date from his time. With Raleigh locked up in the Tower of London, James I sold the estate to the Digby family, who still own it. Further wings were added over the years to create a romantic stately home, filled with works of art, fine furniture and porcelain collections. The extensive gardens, park and lake were laid out by "Capability" Brown in the 1750s. Open from April to October; the Castle hosts several special events during the year.

5. Sherborne Steam and Waterwheel Centre (page 49) at Castleton was set up to preserve a large waterwheel which supplied water to the town from 1869 to 1959. Steam engines and other water supply artefacts make this unusual museum an interesting visit. Open on Sundays and occasional other days May to October.

6. Blackmore Vale (page 48) is a wide valley stretching across northern Dorset between the Dorset Downs in the south and the River Stour watershed to the north. This green landscape still has many small farms, pretty little villages and winding lanes. The varied geology of limestone and clay add variety to this low-lying fertile area.

7. Cerne Abbas (page 44) is situated on the A352 about midway between Sherborne and Dorchester. The village has fascinating old buildings, including a 14th century doorway, a 13th century church and remains of the abbey. The "Royal Oak" claims to be the oldest pub in England.

8. The Cerne Giant (page 44) is on the southwest corner of Giant Hill, just north of the village. Although it can be seen from the official parking place, there is a much better view from Weam Common Hill, reached by a path just opposite.

9. Minterne Gardens (page 45) is 2mi (3km) north of Cerne Abbas. The gardens are in a small valley below the house, with ponds, waterfalls and streams. They are open from mid-February until early November. There is a successive profusion of colour from early spring onwards.

10. Roman Road (page 54) The A37 from Dorchester to Ilchester follows the line of a Roman road for most of the way. At Dorchester the Roman road runs close to the Roman aqueduct before crossing the river, west of Stratton.

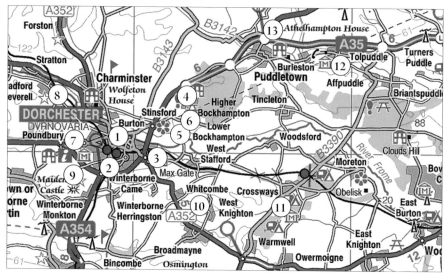

Dorchester (popn. 2011, 19,060) is the county town of Dorset. Though far from being its largest settlement, it makes up for this with a long history and a wide range of places to visit and things to do. From Jurassic fossils to the famous author, Thomas Hardy, Dorcester will repay a visit.

Around 4,000BC, Neolithic people built huge circular henges at the Maumbury Rings and Mount Pleasant. They also built the first enclosure at Maiden Castle. During the Iron Age this was developed into a massive hillfort.

The Romans called the town *Durnovaria*, probably an adaptation of its local name. The High Street follows the original Roman road from Old Sarum to Exeter. Much remains to be seen from these times, including a town house, an impressive aqueduct and parts of the town walls. The museum houses large mosaics as well as many artefacts; artistic, domestic and military.

Development of Dorchester to the north has always been constrained by the River Frome and its flood plain. Like many other towns, it suffered several devastating fires. Those of 1613 and 1725 destroyed most of the town. It was only in the 19th century that Dorchester expanded outside the ancient town walls to the south and east. Today a ring road keeps through traffic out of the town. To the west the "urban village" of Poundbury is continuously expanding.

Dorchester offers shopping, eating out, accommodation and other services greater than might be expected for a small town. There are the usual chain stores, but also many independent specialist shops. With eight museums in the town and numerous attractions roundabout there is plenty to see and do regardless of the season.

Thomas Hardy spent most of his life in or near *"Casterbridge"* as he called the town in his novels. His birthplace at Higher Bockhampton and his residence from 1885, Max Gate, are both National Trust properties. A star attraction in the Dorset County Museum is Hardy's study, complete with his desk, books and pens.

ORDNANCE SURVEY 1:50,000 & 1:25,000 MAPS
OS Landranger Map 194 - Dorchester & Weymouth
OS Explorer Map OL15 - Purbeck & South Dorset

DORCHESTER & AROUND

1. Dorchester (page 54) is a compact town, best explored on foot. There are plenty of convenient car parks as well as two train stations.

The Town Walks (page 56) follow the line of the Roman walls. They enclose many of the sites of interest mentioned here.

Dorset County Museum (page 56) is perhaps the best place to start a visit to the town. It has major displays on Jurassic Coast fossils, archaeology, Dorchester, rural life and, of course, Thomas Hardy.

The Old Crown Court and Cells (page 56) are preserved in Stratton House, High West Street. It was here that the Tolpuddle Martyrs were tried and sentenced in 1834 (page 68).

The Bloody Assizes (page 57) were held in the Antelope Hotel in 1685 after the failed Monmouth Rebellion. The building is now a restaurant.

St Peter's Church (page 56), down the street from the Museum, is one of very few medieval buildings in the town; it dates from the 15th century.

The Keep Military Museum (page 57) is housed in a prominent Victorian mock keep near the Top of the Town roundabout. It covers the history of the Devon and Dorset Regiment from 1685.

The Roman Townhouse (page 54) is behind County Hall, near the Top of the Town roundabout. It is the only such house in the UK.

Hangman's Cottage (page 58) is below Colliton Park beside the Millstream. In former times its tenant was kept busy by the nearby courts.

Small Museums (page 59) There are four small museums to the south of the High Street.

The Dinosaur Museum is a superb hands-on experience which is great for children.

The Tutankhamen Exhibition has a replica of the pharoah's tomb as found in 1922 as well as authentic reconstructions of many artefacts found there.

The Terracotta Warriors Museum has replicas of the famous Chinese clay army.

The Teddy Bear Museum is upstairs and features bears of all types including famous ones such as Paddington Bear and Rupert Bear.

Napper's Mite Almshouse (page 60) in South Street was built in 1616 and is now a restaurant.

2. Maumbury Rings (page 54), near Dorchester South Train Station was originally a Neolithic henge monument. Later, the Romans used it as an amphitheatre, while it was turned into a gun battery during the Civil War. Finally it became the site of public executions, either by hanging or burning.

3. Max Gate (page 62) is just off the junction of the A35 with the A352, east of the town. Hardy lived here from 1885 until his death in 1928.

4. Hardy's Cottage, Higher Bockhampton (page 62), is the birthplace of Hardy. The cottage and its lovely garden are owned by the National Trust.

Stinsford Churchyard (page 62) is off the A35, east of the town. Hardy's heart and both of his wives are buried here.

5. Kingston Maurward House (page 66) near Stinsford, has fine formal gardens and an animal park.

6. Thorncombe Wood (page 66) has a well-preserved section of Roman road. This starts near the carpark, which also give access to Hardy's Cottage

Puddletown Forest (page 66), further east, has a further long section which can be explored.

7. Poundbury (page 61) is on the west side of Dorchester. This new urban village development is very much the creation of HRH Charles, Prince of Wales.

8. A Roman Aqueduct (page 54) once ran from near the Top of the Town roundabout for 12mi (19km) above the River Frome. Its course can be followed from Poundbury hillfort along the side road that follows the Roman road to the northwest.

9. Maiden Castle (page 64), about 2mi (3km) from the town centre, is the largest and most spectacular of Dorset's Iron Age hillforts. Not to be missed, it is accessed by a side road off the Weymouth Road.

10. Whitcombe Church (page 65) on the A352 to Wareham, was for many years the charge of William Barnes, the great poet, philologist and minister.

11. The Mill House Cider Museum (page 67), between Moreton and Owermoigne, has displays of old cider-making equipment and a plant nursery.

12. Tolpuddle Martyrs Museum (page 12), off the A35, tells the story of the farmworkers sentenced to transportation to Australia, but ultimately pardoned in an early success for workers' rights.

13. Athelhampton House & Gardens (page 66) is considered to be one of the best manor houses in the country. It is off the A35 east of Puddletown. It is open all year, but only on Sundays in winter.

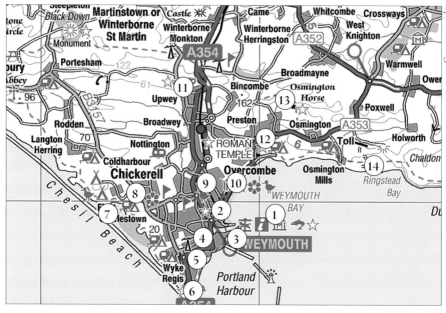

WEYMOUTH (popn. 2011, 52,323) is situated on a peninsula, sheltered from the north by the Ridgeway, from the west by Chesil Beach and, from the south, by Portland. The estuary of the River Wey, already a port during the Iron Age, was developed by the Romans as a military and commercial deep water harbour. Later it became a major commercial port, trading with Europe and North America. Some of the earliest emigrants left from here in the 1620s.

Seaside Resorts were becoming very popular with the rich by the late 1700s. Weymouth, with its long sheltered sandy beach, mild climate and good harbour, developed rapidly after King George III became an enthusiastic visitor. The Georgian and Regency style houses on the Esplanade were built for wealthy businessmen and their families who flocked to this newly upmarket and fashionable resort.

Apart from its fine beach, Weymouth has a great deal to offer today's visitors. Its compact size means everything is within walking distance of the centre. The shopping precinct is partially pedestrianised, while the towns offers a huge range of hotels, guest houses, restaurants, pubs, traditional fish and chips and many small shops selling traditional seaside wares.

Royal Navy developments greatly affected Weymouth from the 1860s, with the construction of the Nothe Fort. The Whitehead Torpedo Works were established in Wyke Regis 1891, immediately creating a demand for skilled labour. During WWII it employed about 1,600 people, producing up to 20 torpedoes per week. It finally shut down in 1997.

Annual Events include Weymouth Carnival, Dorset Seafood Festival, Weymouth Beach MotoX and the Sand Sculpture Festival. Weymouth Pavilion has live performances throughout the year. In keeping with being a year-round resort, Weymouth offers something for everyone whatever the season.

ORDNANCE SURVEY 1:50,000 & 1:25,000 MAPS

OS Landranger Map 194	Dorchester & Weymouth
OS Explorer Map OL15	Purbeck & South Dorset

WEYMOUTH

1. Weymouth (page 72) is situated in a beautiful sheltered position overlooking Weymouth Bay. With its beautiful long sandy beach and many facilities, the town is a fine and popular seaside resort.

2. Weymouth Harbour (page 75) remains a working ferry and fishing port with a large marina upstream. The quaysides have many interesting old buildings, shops, pubs and restaurants, as well as boats and anglers to watch.

The Esplanade (page 74) was mostly built between 1780 and 1850 by rich Londoners. Today this elegant curve of buildings is largely hotels and guest houses with shops and offices below.

The George III Statue (page 74) was erected in 1810 in the King's honour to celebrate his 50th Jubilee on the throne. He still surveys the Esplanade from his high plinth.

The Jubilee Clock (page 74) on the Esplanade celebrates Queen Victoria's 50th year in office in 1887. Both the statue and the clock were renovated for the 2012 Olympic Games.

The Shopping Precinct (page 75) is partly pedestrianised. Apart from the ubiquitous chain stores it has a wide choice of independent shops, ranging from upmarket fashion and jewellery stores to outlets selling seaside resort goods.

The Pleasure Pier (page 76) is dominated by the Weymouth Sea Life Tower. The viewing capsule commands fine panoramic views over the town.

Sand Sculptures (page 74) have been a feature on the beach near the Pleasure Pier for over 90 years.

Tudor House Museum (page 75) in Trinity Street dates from the 17th century. The nearby Old Rooms are an even older merchant's house.

3. The Nothe Fort (page 80) was originally built as a gun battery by Henry VIII. The current impressive fort dates from the 1860s and houses a fascinating military museum. There are many military artefacts from over 100 years of usage of the site.

4. Melcombe Regis (page 72), north of the harbour is the oldest part of town. The first town bridge was built in 1594. Originally Weymouth was the settlement on the south side of the harbour.

5. Wyke Regis (page 76) is the former industrial part of Weymouth, now mostly housing estates.

The Rodwell Trail (page 76) follows a disused railway line from Weymouth Harbour to Ferry Bridge. There are fine views across Weymouth Bay.

Sandsfoot Castle (page 76) is a "device fort" built by Henry VIII off the Rodwell Trail. The ruins of this large gun platform have recently been stabilised.

6. Ferry Bridge (page 76) spans the Fleet estuary. The first bridge was built in 1839, while the current one dates from 1985.

7. Chesil Beach (page 76) is a shingle barrier beach, stretcheing 18mi (29km) from West Bay to Portland. It is up to 200m wide and 15m high and is very hard walking.

East Fleet (page 76) is the southern half of the Fleet Lagoon. The *"Fleet Observer"* runs boat trips here in summer. The South West Coast Path follows the beach from Ferry Bridge to Langton Herring.

Fleet (page 78) inspired the novel *Moonfleet*. The Fleet can be accessed in several places near here, including via the romantic Moonfleet Manor Hotel.

8. Bennett's Water Gardens (page 78) are 2mi (3km) west of the town centre on the B3157. Former clay pits have been imaginatively redeveloped and landscaped into a delightful exotic fairyland.

9. Radipole Lake RSPB Reserve (page 77) is a large area of lakes and wetland northwest of the harbour. There is a visitor centre, several hides, boardwalks and a choice of trails.

10. Lodmoor Country Park (page 77) has a host of attractions including Weymouth Sea Life Park.

Lodmoor RSPB Reserve (page 77) is another wetland site with several hides and nature trails.

11. Upwey Wishing Well (page 74) off the A354 north of Weymouth, was regularly visited by George III and is the source of the short River Wey.

12. Jordan Hill Roman Temple (page 72) is signposted off Furzy Cliff road above Bowleaze Cove northwest of the town. Only the footings remain.

13. The Osmington White Horse (page 79) is carved into the chalk of White Horse Hill. Said to represent George III leaving Weymouth it is best viewed from the A353 west of Osmington.

14. Ringstead Bay (page 79) is overlooked by the dramatic chalk cliffs of the White Nothe and Burning Cliff. This lovely shingle and sand beach can be reached by toll road off the A353 or by footpath from the National Trust White Nothe carpark.

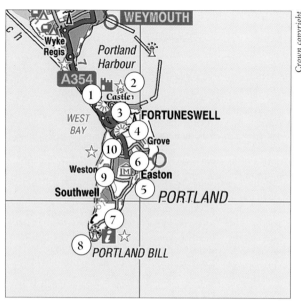

The Isle of Portland (popn. 2011, 12,844) is 4mi (6km) long by 1.5mi (2.5km) wide. Until 1839 the only access was by a small ferry over the Fleet estuary, or by sea. As a result the Portlanders had an island culture, and referred to incomers as *"kimberlin"*.

From Saxon times until the 19th century Portland was a Royal Manor, under the Crown and not the local authority. The ancient system of land tenure still holds today in Southwell, where narrow strips of land can be seen fenced off near Portland Bill.

Portland Sheep (page 197) were once the main agricultural product, both for their fine wool and exceptional meat. By the mid 1800s over 4,000 lambs were exported every year. The last flock was sold in 1920, and the breed nearly died out but is once more in demand and no longer threatened.

Quarrying for Portland Stone has been a major industry here since Roman times. This easily worked,

but erosion-resistant, stone has been much used in London and elsewhere for centuries. Extraction continues today, mostly by mining, and not open cast quarrying. The numerous abandoned quarries are now given over to nature. Many limestone-loving plants and insects thrive here. These include Portland Sea-lavender and Spurge as well as rare butterflies such as the Adonis, Chalkhill and Silver-studded Blues.

Portland Harbour was developed into a huge, sprawling naval base by the Royal Navy between 1860 and 1892. This took over a large part of the north of the Isle for the gun batteries, harbour works, accommodation blocks, workers' housing and the essential HM Prison. Vast quarries were opened up to supply the stone for the forts, piers and breakwaters. The harbour proved untenable in both WWI and WWII and was abandoned completely by the Royal Navy in 1999.

Portland Bill was a major hazard for shipping due to its tide race and associated eddies. The Shambles, a large sandbank to the southeast, claimed many ships. Lyme Bay, with its adverse currents, was also a serious danger for sailing ships. The first two lights were lit in 1716 and replaced by the present tower in 1906.

The southern tip of Portland remains much as it has for centuries, with its field system of *"lawnsheds"*, small coastal quarries and a general lack of development. It seems a world apart from the now-abandoned 19th century military installations and their associated sprawling quarries. The South West Coast Path circumnavigates the Isle of Portland, taking in the Portland Heights viewpoint and Portland Bill.

ORDNANCE SURVEY 1:50,000 & 1:25,000 MAPS
OS Landranger Map 194   Dorchester & Weymouth
OS Explorer Map OL15   Purbeck & South Dorset

The Isle of Portland

1. The Isle of Portland (page 82) is a massive limestone plateau joined to the Mainland by Chesil Beach and Ferry Bridge. There is much to interest visitors in a small area, including its unique landscape, history and wildlife.

2. Portland Harbour (page 84) is protected by massive breakwaters and three huge forts. It encloses c.520ha. Today it is a commercial port.

Mulberry Harbour (page DGB 105) Two unused caissons from the WWII Mulberry Harbours now provide shelter at Portland Harbour.

Osprey Quay (page DGB 104), the former site of *HMS Osprey* Royal Naval Air Station, has been comprehensively redeveloped since the RN left in 1999. With a large marina and many marine-based companies, the site continues to be expanded.

Weymouth & Portland National Sailing Academy (pages 82) was the official host of the 2012 Olympic Games sailing events.

Portland Castle (page 82) is a "Device Fort" built by Henry VIII in 1539. It has been restored to its Tudor form and includes the Captain's Garden and Tearoom. It is maintained by English Heritage and open from April to October.

3. Fortuneswell (page 83) dates mostly from Victorian times, when its attractive rows of terraced houses were built. The village makes an interesting circular walk, but the hills are steep.

Verne Yeates Viewpoint (page 83) at Portland Heights offers a panoramic view over the whole of Chesil Beach and Weymouth Bay to Purbeck. On a clear day this is one of the best views in Dorset.

4. The Verne Citadel (page 84) is not open to the public. This former HM Prison is now an "Immigration Removal Centre." The formidable entrance and parts of the exterior are visible.

Verne High Angle Battery (page 85), to the east of Portland Heights, is open to the public. There are many tunnels to explore with a torch, as well as gun positions. Now a nature reserve, along with the East Weares Battery, this is an excellent place to look for wild flowers and butterflies in the summer.

5. Easton (page 86), the centre of Portland, has many attractive quarrymen's cottages, built of the local stone. There are Portland Stone quarries all around, some of which are still in operation.

St George's Church (page 86) is prominent in the centre of Portland. This large Grade I listed building is well worth visiting. Some consider it to be the most accomplished 18th century church in Dorset. The nearby George Inn dates from 1797.

Portland Museum (page 86) in Wakeham is housed in two small 17th century cottages. It covers Portland Stone, fossils, people, the sea and prisons.

Church Ope Cove (page) is reached from a path near the museum. In former times this attractive little bay was a fishing station.

Rufus Castle (page 87) was originally built in the 11th century by William II and much modified over the centuries. It is now ruinous.

Pennsylvania Castle (page 87), now an exclusive hotel, was built by John Penn, grandson of William Penn, the founder of Pennsylvania c.1800.

6. Broadcroft Quarry Butterfly Reserve (page 90) at Easton is one of several nature reserves on Portland dedicated to butterflies and wild flowers which prefer calcareous soils. Others include King Barrow, Perryfield and Tout Quarries.

7. Culverwell (page 88), near Portland Bill is the only Mesolithic site in Dorset where there is anything to see - in this case the remains of stone floors and walls dating from c.6000BC.

8. Portland Bill (page 88) is the most southerly point on Dorset. The current lighthouse is open to the public. The whole southern part of the Isle can be explored via the coastal path and many inland trails. In summer this is a wonderful place for butterflies and wild flowers, while during spring and autumn this is one of the best places to seek migrant birds in Dorset.

Portland Bird Observatory (page 88) is housed in the Old Lower Lighthouse.

9. Weston (page 87), a westwards extension of Easton, offers access to the west coast, including the spectacular cliffs at Blacknor and Mutton Cove.

10. Tout Quarry Sculpture Park (page 90), above West Weare, has many sculptures to search for in its abandoned workings, as well as butterflies.

Large Skipper at Powerstock Common

Dorset Bibliography

DORSET - GENERAL BOOKS

Title	Author	Publisher	Year
Slow Dorset	Alexandra Richards	Bradt	2012
Beautiful Dorset	Salmon	J Salmon Ltd	
Dorset, The Complete Guide	Jo Draper	Dovecote Press	2003
Dorset, Hampshire & the Isle of Wight	Hancock & Tomlin	Rough Guides	2013
The Dorset Coast	Adam Burton	Frances Lincoln	2008
Dorset Visitors Guide	Richard Sale	Landmark	2007
The Dorset Landscape	John Chaffey	Dorset Books	2004
Dorset	Richard Ollard	Dovecote	1999
Dorset	Oeta Whaley	Venton	2002
Dorset's World Heritage Coast	John Beavis	Tempus	2004
Curious Dorset	Derrick Warren	Sutton Publishing	2004
Portland Sheep	Norman Jones	Norman Jones	
Official Dorset Miniguide	ed Helen Baker	Compass Maps	2012

WALKING

Title	Author	Publisher	Year
50 Walks in Dorset	AF Stonehouse	AA Publishing	2013
Dorset Walks	Coduit, Brooks & Viccars	Jarrold	2006
Dorset Rubber Stamp Pub Walks	Kemp & Clarke	Clarke Publications	1992
Exploring the Undercliffs	Donald Campbell	Coastal Publishing	2006
Holloway	Macfarlane et al	Faber & Faber	2013
A Boot Up Mid Dorset	Rodney Legg	PiZX Books	2011
A Boot Up Dorset's Jurassic Coast	Rodney Legg	PiZX Books	2008

ARCHAEOLOGY

Title	Author	Publisher	Year
Dorset's Archaeology	Peter Stanier	Dorset Books	2004
Prehistoric Dorset	John Gale	Tempus Publishing	2003
Ancient Stones of Dorset	Peter Knight	Power Publications	1996
In Search of the Durotriges	Martin Papworth	History Press	2011
Roman Dorset	Bill Putnam	History Press	2007

HISTORY - GENERAL

Title	Author	Publisher	Year
A History of Dorset	CE Cullingford	Phillimore	1999
Dorset's Best Churches	B Lehane & D Bailey	Dovecote	2006
Dorset, West Country History	Peta Whaley	Venton	2002
Saxons & Vikings	David A Hinton	Dovecote Press	1998
Somerset & Dorset Railway	Robin Atthill	David & Charles	1985
Dorset in the Age of Steam	Peter Stanier	Dorset Books	2002
Dorset The Royal Navy	Stuart Morris	Dovecote	2011
Dorset The Army	George Forty	Dovecote	2011
Dorset The Royal Air Force	Colin Pomeroy	Dovecote	2011

HISTORY - SPECIFIC PLACES

Title	Author	Publisher	Year
Wodetone, A Wooded Place	Guy Bryan	Wootton 2000 Group	2004
Bridport Past	Gerard Gosling	Biddles	1999
Bridport & West Bay, Flax & Hemp	Mike Williams	English Heritage	2006
The Cerne Giant	Rodney Castleden	Dorset Publishing Co	1996
Lyme Regis Pocket Guide	Steve Postles	Steve Postles	1979
Portland	Stuart Morris	Dovecote Press	1998

PLACENAMES AND LANGUAGE

The Place-Names of Dorset	Anton Fagersten	Uppsala	1933
Dorset Place-Names	AD Mills	Countryside Books	1998

GEOLOGY AND FOSSILS

Fossils & Rocks of the Jurassic Coast	Robert Westwood	Inspiring Places	2008
Geology of the Jurassic Coast, Exmouth to Lyme Regis	Richard A Edwards	Coastal Publishing	2008
Fossil Hunters of Charmouth	Lesley Dunlop	Shoreline	2010
Kingcombe Meadows Nature Reserve	Dorset Wildlife Trust		
Wildlife of the Jurassic Coast	Bryan Edwards	Coastal Publishing	2008
Discover Dorset, Geology	Paul Ensom	Dovecote Press	1998

NATURAL HISTORY - GENERAL

Natural History of Dorset	Dorset Wildlife Trust	Dovecote Press	1997
Dorset, A Naturalist's County	Nigel Webb & Tony Bates	Dovecote Press	2011
D			

NATURAL HISTORY - BIRDS

Collins Bird Guide	Mullarney et al	HarperCollins	2000
Best Birdwatching Sites in Dorset	Neil Gartshore	Buckingham Press	2011
Where to Watch Birds in Dorset, Hampshire and IOW	G Green & M Cade	Helm	2010

NATURAL HISTORY - INSECTS

Britain's Butterflies	Newland, Still et al	WILDGuides	2010
Dragonflies and Damselflies	Brooks and Lewington	British Wildlife Publishing	2004
Britain's Dragonflies	D Smallshire & A Swash	WILDGuides	2014

NATURAL HISTORY - FLORA

Wild Flowers of Britain & Ireland	Blamey, Fitter & Fitter	A&C Black	2003
Orchids of Britain & Ireland	Anne & Simon Harrap	A&C Black	2005
Discovering Dorset's Wild Flowers	Peter Cramb	P&M Cramb	2013
Wild Flowers of the Dorset Coast Path	Cramb & Cramb	P&M Cramb	2003
Wild Flower Walks in Dorset	Cramb & Cramb	P&M Cramb	2006
Shorter Wild Flower Walks in Dorset	Cramb & Cramb	P&M Cramb	2009
The Wild Flowers of Dorset	Stuart Roberts	Dovecote	1984

MAPS

OS Landranger	Map 183	Yeovil & Frome	Ordnance Survey	2005
OS Landranger	Map 193	Taunton & Lyme Regis	Ordnance Survey	2003
OS Landranger	Map 194	Dorchester & Weymouth	Ordnance Survey	2007
OS Explorer	Map OL15	Purbeck & South Dorset	Ordnance Survey	2010
OS Explorer	Map 116	Lyme Regis & Bridport	Ordnance Survey	2011
OS Explorer	Map 117	Cerne Abbas & Bere Regis	Ordnance Survey	2010
OS Explorer	Map 129	Yeovil & Sherborne	Ordnance Survey	2010

Index

SOUTHERN RAILWAY.

THIS BIT OF COAST COMMENCES JUST EAST OF LYME REGIS (DORSET) AND EXTENDS PAST THE LANDSLIP (DEVON), SEATON, SIDMOUTH, BUDLEIGH SALTERTON TO EXMOUTH, WITH DARTMOOR IN THE BACKGROUND. IT IS TYPICAL OF THE MANY CHARMING HOLIDAY REGIONS TO WHICH THE SOUTHERN RAILWAY PROVIDES ACCESS BY EXPRESS RESTAURANT CAR TRAINS.

1923 Southern Railways poster

West Dorset Guide Book 1ˢᵗ edition by Charles Tait

Index

Charmouth Beach at a very low tide

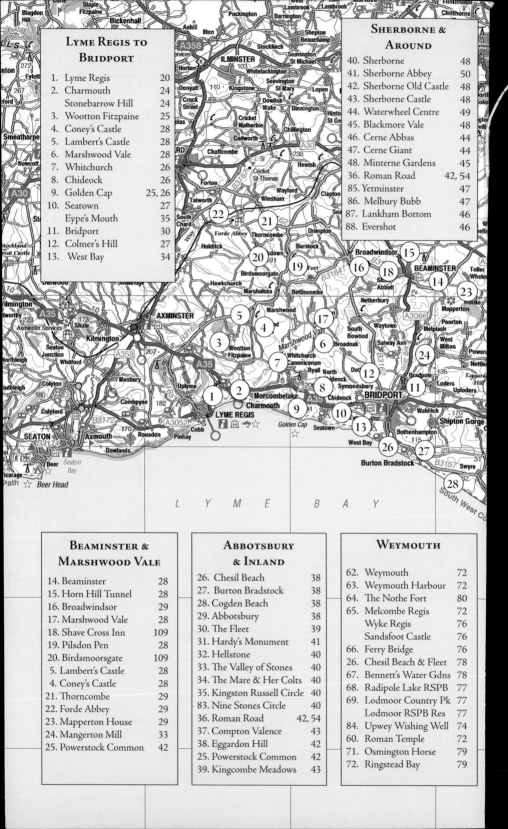